PRACTICAL
JAPANESE COOKING

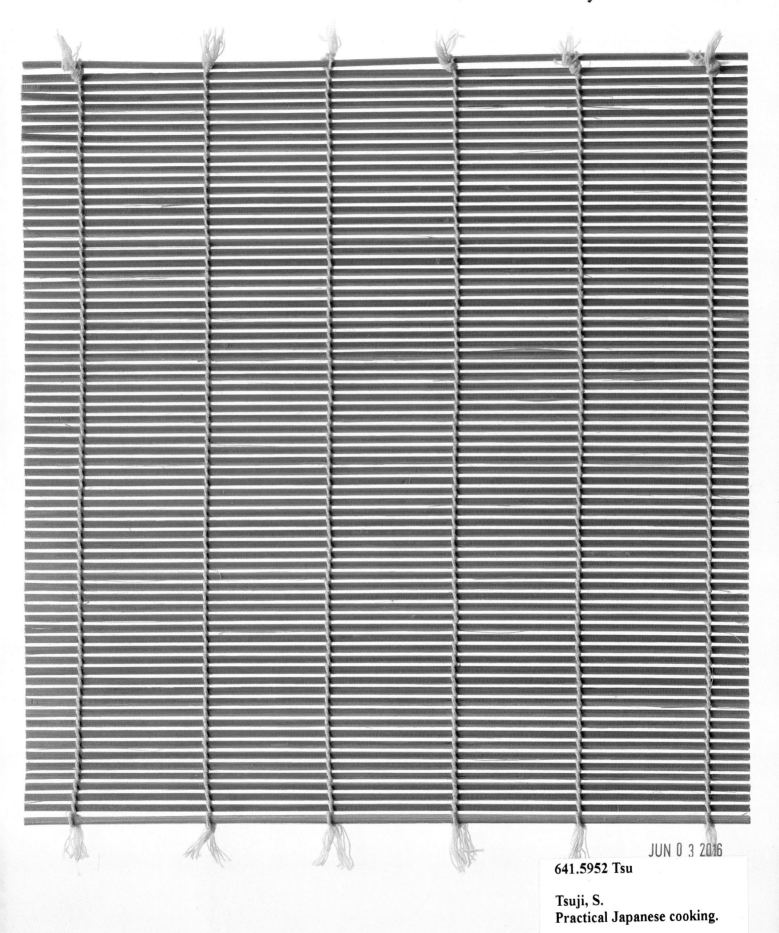

KODANSHA USA

PRACTICAL JAPANESE COOKING

Easy and Elegant

Shizuo Tsuji

Koichiro Hata

New Foreword by
David Bouley

New Preface by
Yoshiki Tsuji

Photographs by
Yoshikatsu Saeki

Calories are per serving or per unit.

Process photographs by Kazuyoshi Koshiba and Toshiki Konishi

The authors and publisher wish to thank Suntory Ltd. for its support.

The publisher would like to thank the following for donating tableware: Diners House; Dodwell & Co., Ltd.; Ejiry; Fujikigyo Co., Ltd.; Ginza Blume; Hoshi Shoji Ltd.; Nikko Co.; Noritake Sales Co., Ltd.; Ohmukai Koshudo Co., Ltd.; Royal Copenhagen Japan Ltd.; Sasaki Crystal; Seito Co., Ltd.; Suita Trading Co., Ltd.; Tachikichi Inc.; Ueno International Co., Ltd.; Wado Shoji K.K.; and Wedgwood Japan Ltd.

Published by Kodansha USA, Inc.
451 Park Avenue South
New York, NY 10016

Distributed in the United Kingdom and continental Europe
by Kodansha Europe Ltd.

Printed in South Korea through Dai Nippon Printing Co., Ltd.
ISBN 978-1-56836-567-1

First edition published in Japan in 1986 by Kodansha International
First US edition 2016 by Kodansha USA

21 20 19 18 17 16   6 5 4 3 2 1

www.kodanshausa.com

CONTENTS

Preface 7

APPETIZERS

Skewered Omelette, Cucumber, and
    Shrimp 10
Rolled Flounder with Egg 11
Stuffed Minced-Chicken Rolls 12
Sautéed Duck Breast with Sauce 13
Steamed Abalone 14
Jellied Shrimp and Sea Urchin 15
Grilled Squid with Golden Topping and
    Oil-Grilled Green Peppers 16
Shimeji Mushrooms with Pine
    Needles 16
Shrimp and Sardine Rafts 17
Endive Boats with Avocado, Crab, and
    Salmon Roe 18
Squid and Asparagus with Mustard-Miso
    Sauce 19
Jade Green Deep-Fried Shrimp 19

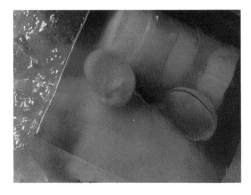

SOUP

Crab Ball Soup 20
Clam Soup 22
Chicken Ball and Cucumber Soup 22
Tofu, Pork, and Vegetable Soup 24
Pureed Corn Soup 24
Miso Soup with Pork and Vegetables 25
Scallop and Vegetable Soup 25

FISH

Quick-Seared Bonito Sashimi 26
Tuna Sashimi with Grated Radish 28
Paper-Thin Sea Bass Sashimi 29
Night-Dried Sole 30
Deep-Fried Flounder Boat 30
Deep-Fried Sea Bass 32
Simmered Rockfish 32
Yuan-Style Grilled Butterfish 34
Yellowtail Teriyaki 35
Sardines Simmered with Ginger 36
Simmered Mackerel in Miso 37
Stuffed Salmon 38
Deep-Fried Trout in Vegetable Sauce 39

SEAFOOD

Stuffed Spiny Lobster 40
Saké-Simmered Lobster 42
Whole Prawns Grilled in the Shell 42
Squid Teriyaki 44
Clams Grilled in the Shell 45
Vinegared Crab 46
Shrimp and Leeks with Mustard-Miso
    Sauce 48
Scallops and Kiwi Fruit with Three-Flavors
    Dressing 49

BEEF AND PORK

Grilled Beef 50
Beef Tartare, Japanese Style 52
Grilled Beef with Miso 54
Simmered Beef with Vegetables 55
Rolled Beef and Asparagus 56
Beef Salad 57
Nagasaki-Style Braised Pork 58
Deep-Fried Stuffed Pork 59

CHICKEN

Yakitori 60
Soft-Simmered Chicken 62
Chicken Escabeche Nanban 63
Tatsuta Fried Chicken 64
Chicken, Grapefruit, and Corn Salad with
    Almond Dressing 65

EGG

Savory Custard Cup 66
Wrapped Custard 68
Japanese Coddled Egg 69

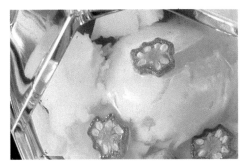

TOFU

Simmered Tofu   70
Night-Dried Tofu with Chicken Sauce   72
Simmered Tofu Dumplings   73
Deep-Fried Tofu   75
Scrambled Tofu   76
White Salad   77
Tofu Sandwiches   78
Tofu Hamburger Steak   80
Freeze-Dried Tofu with Egg   81

VEGETABLES

Stuffed Potato Buns   82
Grilled Eggplant   84
Deep-Fried Eggplant with Miso Sauce   85
Deep-Fried Eggplant Sandwiches   86
Vegetable-and-Shrimp Clusters   87
Turnip with Ginger-Miso Sauce   88
Steamed Grated Turnip   88
Chinese Cabbage and Deep-Fried
   Tofu   90
Stuffed Cabbage, Japanese Style   91
Simmered Bamboo Shoot with *Wakame*
   Seaweed   92
Deep-Fried and Simmered Acorn
   Squash   93
Simmered Soybeans   94
Deep-Fried Zucchini   94
Sautéed Celery with Sesame   94
Vegetables with White Sesame
   Dressing   96
Marinated Watercress   96
Okra and Coddled Egg with *Wasabi*
   Sauce   97
Spinach with Sesame Dressing   97

RICE

Rice Balls   98
Mixed Rice   100
Chicken and Egg on Rice   101

SUSHI

Decorative Sushi   102
Scattered Sushi   106
Bo Sushi   108
Nigiri Sushi   110
Thick Roll Sushi   113
Inari Sushi   114

NOODLES

Chilled *Somen* Noodles   116
Udon Pot   118
Soba Noodles in a Basket   120
Udon Noodles with Deep-Fried Tofu   120
Soba Noodles with Duck   121

ONE-POT DISHES

Sukiyaki   122
Oden Stew   124
Seafood Pot   126

OTHER DELECTABLES

Savory Pancake   128
Tempura   130
Deep-Fried Mixed Kebabs   132

BOX MEAL   134
SHOKADO BOX MEAL   137

Cooking Tips   140

Ingredients   144

Index   150

PREFACE

It is well known that Japanese food, with the attention given to arrangement, pleases the eye as well as the palate. It is almost equally well known that it can reach elegant and exotic heights or can be as humble as a porridge. But what most often escapes notice is the fact that this many-faceted cooking tradition relies heavily on two primary ingredients—delicate bonito stock (*dashi*) and, not unexpectedly, soy sauce. Most, if not all, dishes call for one or both. In addition, every dish shares a single basic but all-important requirement: unstinting freshness. Knowing this, cooking Japanese becomes little more than choosing from the abundance of in-season foods (not frozen seafood or hothouse grown vegetables) that your grocer has to offer—fish, meat, greens, whatever.

Japanese cooking is nothing if not versatile. The Japanese ambiance of the food in these pages is not lost though the majority of the meals are displayed on Western plates. By the same token, the food loses nothing with innovation. As a pianist may incorporate a cadenza in a Mozart concerto during a live performance, so may the recipes here be improvised on, played with, adapted to personal tastes in the kitchen arena. We all follow our instincts when we cook, so in a very real sense, we are artists. Once you have "understood" the food here—and it is no difficult or profound matter—let your culinary impulses take over. Mold Japanese meals to suit your mood—they will not lose their "Japaneseness." On the contrary, they will gain an immeasurable something that might be called the melding of cultures, ideas, or some such. Or try adding a Japanese accent to a few of your often-made dishes or inserting your own favorite foods into a typical Japanese recipe. Play with presentation as the urge strikes you.

Daily, there are new signs of a slow but steady merging of world cultures and of cuisines. At the very least, with each passing year there is a greater borrowing of ideas. Japanese cooking has much still to offer. Here is Japanese food that can be savored. As the title suggests, practicality and ease are stressed, but the charm is not lost. Explore and dig out what you like. Treat yourself, family, and friends to a touch of Japan, a new dining experience, new refreshing tastes. Then sit back and enjoy it. For food, family, and friends are meant to be enjoyed in just that way. The pleasure of good company and good food is something shared among all countries everywhere.

Shizuo Tsuji

NEW PREFACE

More than 50 years ago, Japanese cuisine was introduced to the USA and other countries, and has since spread. It has had an immense influence on world cuisine, and in recent years, it has experienced a worldwide boom. It has gradually moved away from being a merely "exotic" cuisine, to one where its unique aesthetics, tastes, and textures are appreciated by more and more people. Even within homes and the professional hospitality business, Japanese cuisine has started to take its place alongside traditional Western cooking. It has been estimated that there will be 55,000 Japanese restaurants throughout the world within three years.

The first edition of this book by my father, Shizuo Tsuji, was published in 1986, and it was his second book introducing Japanese cooking to readers outside Japan. The first title, *Japanese Cooking: A Simple Art* (1980), discussed the values and aesthetics underlying Japanese cuisine, together with explanations of cooking utensils, such as kitchen knives, and the unique ingredients that are used in Japanese cooking. It also introduced many standard recipes to the reader. He had a strong desire to convey the spirit of his country's food culture in the same way as French cuisine is regarded overseas. The book has become a classic in the literature of Japanese cooking in English, and is still referred to by many readers.

As you can see from the title of this second book, it aims to be a more practical and less theoretical guide than the first. An important part of what makes it so practical, however, is Shizuo Tsuji's intention to show that Japanese cuisine is both versatile and adaptable. He understood that when home cooks outside of Japan prepare Japanese dishes, it's very possible that some ingredients, equipment, techniques, or tastes will be different. He felt that he should keep the recipes as authentic as possible to preserve and convey the basic concepts underlying Japanese food. But he encouraged cooks to take the original recipes and add, subtract, or change them in ways that make them their own.

To that end, the dishes here used modern Western tableware and were selected to meet Western tastes, but still retained the essence of Japanese cuisine. When the proposal was made to republish this book in a soft-cover edition, I originally thought that the contents should be updated to include some more recent contemporary recipes. But rather than take advantage of recent changes, which may prove to be only fads, it was decided to keep the original contents. By following these recipes, professional and amateur cooks alike can recreate the authentic taste of Japanese food.

Diners in just about every corner of the globe have the opportunity to eat some sort of Japanese food. Whether it's at a neighborhood *izakaya*, a Michelin-starred restaurant, or a sushi counter, the common language and novel taste experience of Japanese cuisine are already there. It is now easier than ever to buy Japanese ingredients, and the barriers to the creation of these recipes have come down. I think it is fair to say that these are good reasons for this book of recipes to be accepted.

Looking at the recipes in this book, you may be struck by an underlying, seemingly simple common structure to their taste — namely, the use of Japanese stock (*dashi*) and soy sauce. This differs from Western cooking. But is it really that simple? In fact, attention to detail here is all. We have been extremely careful in our recipes, with exact measurements of the amount of *dashi* and soy sauce. It will be best to follow the recipes precisely at first, and then adjust the amounts of the ingredients to suit individual tastes.

Lastly, in this book, we are not even attempting to introduce the structure of the "haute cuisine" of Japan, *kaiseki*. This book includes various recipes, ranging from complex recipes reflecting professional techniques and standards, through to easily cooked recipes. This allows you to choose your menus, depending on the ingredients available to you, the structure of the meal, and the occasion at which the meal will be served.

Japanese cuisine both respects tradition and embraces innovation. The subtitle of this book articulates the concepts of ease of preparation combined with elegance. If you can feel the nature of Japanese cuisine from the principles embodied in these recipes, even while they are flexible in their application, this book has served its purpose.

Yoshiki Tsuji

NEW INTRODUCTION

From an early age, I was strongly influenced by life on my grandparents' farm in Connecticut, their French heritage instilling in me a love of the land, an appreciation for fresh products, care in preparation, and the inspiration to cook and enjoy healthful meals.

When I opened my first restaurant in New York in 1987, I based my menus on this approach to food, emphasizing seasonality and a close connection to the ingredients and their sources. This relationship with the farmers and the ingredients was similar to that of a Japanese chef, although I didn't realize how similar until 1996. I had recently closed Bouley Restaurant, and had decided to go to Japan at the invitation of Yoshiki Tsuji, the son of Shizuo Tsuji and the current president of the Tsuji Culinary Institute.

Mr. Tsuji and his colleague Koichiro Hata took me under their wing to teach me Japanese cooking. We went to many different Japanese restaurants, and at each meal, we spoke at length about what we were eating and what I was tasting. This experience was the beginning of my education in Japanese food culture.

Today, more and more chefs in the West are realizing that they can incorporate Japanese techniques and ingredients into their dishes, yet hold on to the distinctive character that makes them their own. This concept is the foundation of Shizuo Tsuji's groundbreaking cookbook.

Practical Japanese Cooking is as relevant now as it was when it was written – perhaps even more so. It's an accessible, welcoming guide to using artisanal ingredients that deliver clear and powerful results in terms of flavor and nutrient density. I know because I see the results every day in my restaurants!

Take the step and be amazed at how accurate and easy the recipes are, and you will find, in the cooking repertoire of Japanese cuisine, a new friend.

David Bouley

Appetizers

Skewered Omelette, Cucumber, and Shrimp

Atsuyaki tamago, kyuri, ebi-umani, kushi-zashi

Lightly sweetened omelette, salted cucumber, and shrimp boiled in the shell make a colorful prelude to any meal.

Makes 20 skewers

THICK OMELETTE

7 oz (200 g) small raw shrimp, shelled and deveined (page 48)

10 egg yolks, lightly beaten

8 whole eggs, lightly beaten

1¼ cups (300 ml) saké, alcohol burned off (page 147)

6 Tbsps sugar

2 Tbsps *mirin*, alcohol burned off (page 146)

1 tsp light soy sauce

⅔ tsp salt

vegetable oil

CUCUMBER

5 Japanese cucumbers or 1 large cucumber

2-inch (5-cm) length kelp (*konbu*)

2 tsps salt

SHRIMP

20 raw shrimp, 1 oz (25 g) each

1⅔ cups (400 ml) bonito stock (*dashi*) (page 140)

½ cup (120 ml) saké

½ cup (120 ml) *mirin*

1 Tbsp light soy sauce

1 Tbsp sugar

pinch salt

20 bamboo skewers

Preheat the oven to 360°–400° F (180°–200° C).

Make the THICK OMELETTE first. Place the shrimp and egg yolk in a food processor and whir to a fine paste (or chop the shrimp as finely as possible, then grind in a mortar and pestle, add egg yolk, and grind again). Remove the mixture to a bowl and gradually mix in the lightly beaten whole egg. Do this gently to avoid creating bubbles. Add the remaining omelette ingredients (except oil), mix thoroughly, and pour through a fine sieve.

Line the bottom and sides of a small (6 × 7-inch/15 × 18-cm), square mold or baking pan with sheets of baking paper cut to fit. Brush with vegetable oil.

Pour the egg batter into the pan to a depth of ¾ inch (2 cm); skim any bubbles from the surface. Line the bottom of a large roasting pan with a kitchen towel and place the pan containing the egg mixture on top. Put the pans in the preheated oven and carefully pour boiling water into the roaster around the egg pan to about half its depth. Bake for 30 minutes. Should the top of the omelette begin to brown or burn while baking, cover the pan with foil. The omelette is done when a toothpick inserted in the center comes out clean.

Unmold and let cool, then cut into ¾-inch (2-cm) cubes.

Rub the Japanese CUCUMBERS with salt and then roll on a cutting board. Drop in boiling water for a few seconds until the color brightens, transfer to cold water, then drain. (If using a regular cucumber, peel, quarter lengthwise, and seed.) Cut into ¾-inch (2-cm) lengths. Combine the kelp and salt with 1¼ cups (300 ml) water and soak the cucumber in this mixture for 15 minutes.

Devein the 20 shrimp (page 48) and set aside. Combine the remaining SHRIMP ingredients in a saucepan and bring to a boil over high heat. Add the shrimp, boil 2 minutes, remove from heat, and let cool in the liquid. Shell the shrimp, leaving the tails intact.

Drain the cucumbers and shrimp thoroughly and skewer them with squares of the omelette.

149 Cals

Rolled Flounder with Egg

Hirame kinshi-maki

Thin slices of vinegared flounder wrapped in paper-thin omelettes marry flavors deliciously when chilled. A dash of Ginger-Vinegar Dressing (page 46) on each roll just before serving adds a pleasing note of sharpness.

Serves 15–20

2 lbs (1 kg) flounder fillets
kelp (*konbu*) reserved from making bonito stock (optional; see To Prepare)

MARINADE

2 cups (480 ml) rice vinegar
⅔ cup (160 ml) water
2 Tbsps sugar
2-inch (5-cm) length kelp (*konbu*)

THIN OMELETTE

5–6 eggs
pinch salt
vegetable oil

STUFFING

1 hard-boiled egg yolk
3–4 stalks green asparagus, trimmed
2 oz (60 g) smoked salmon fillet

bamboo rolling mat (page 143)

TO PREPARE

Sprinkle the fillet with salt and let stand for 1½ hours.

Wash well and drain. Combine all the MARINADE ingredients in a bowl and marinate until the surface of the fillet turns white.

Drain the fish for 1 hour.

Wrap it in kelp left over from making bonito stock. Wrap again in plastic wrap and refrigerate for 5–6 hours.

TO MAKE

Cut the fillet into ⅛-inch (⅔-cm) thick slices.

Make the THIN OMELETTE (page 107), using an 8-inch (20-cm) frying pan. Make 9 sheets. Trim to 6-inch (15-cm) squares (corners will be clipped).

Prepare the STUFFING ingredients: Force the egg yolk through a fine drum sieve, place in a dry saucepan, add a little salt, and parch over low heat until it becomes dry and crumbly. Cook the asparagus in lightly salted water, transfer to cold water, then drain. Cut each stalk lengthwise into 5–6 thin strips. (Make at least 18 strips.) Cut the salmon fillet into thin strips.

Line a bamboo rolling mat with plastic wrap, lay out 1 omelette sheet, and cover the nearer half with thin slices of the flounder. In the center of the flounder make 2 rows of asparagus, and 1 each of the smoked salmon and the parched egg yolk. Working from the near edge, roll the omelette neatly and tightly. Remove the rolling mat and wrap roll (still in plastic) in medium-weight brown paper. Secure with a rubber band or kitchen string. Make 8 more rolls.

Refrigerate for 2 hours.

Remove the plastic wrap and cut rolls into ½-inch (1-cm) rounds before serving.

118 Cals

Lay out asparagus, smoked salmon, and egg yolk on flounder

Roll up from edge closest to you

Press and secure bamboo mat or plastic wrap and brown paper (not shown) with string or rubber band and set aside

Stuffed Minced-Chicken Rolls

Toriniku kenchin-mushi

Try this vegetable-egg mélange rolled in ground chicken for your next party. A platter of this hors d'oeuvre, which has been steamed and then simmered to a mouthwatering sheen, has instant appeal.

Makes 40 pieces

WRAPPING

14 oz (400 g) ground chicken
2 eggs, lightly beaten
1 Tbsp fresh ginger juice (page 145)
2 Tbsps sugar
2 Tbsps dark soy sauce
2 Tbsps saké
2 Tbsps cornstarch dissolved in 2 Tbsps water

STUFFING

1 dried cloud ear mushroom
⅛ medium carrot
4 eggs
1 Tbsp sugar
1 tsp salt
dash light soy sauce

FOR SIMMERING

7 Tbsps saké
2 Tbsps dark soy sauce
1 Tbsp *mirin*
1 Tbsp sugar

ground *sansho* pepper

Make a row of stuffing down center of wrapping

Roll up, secure ends with string, and puncture plastic wrap in several places with toothpick

Soak the cloud ear mushroom for 1 hour (page 142). Cut the mushroom into ⅛-inch (⅓-cm) squares, parboil, refresh in cold water, and drain.

Cut the carrot into small squares the same size as the mushroom, parboil in lightly salted water, refresh in cold water, and drain.

Whir all the WRAPPING ingredients in a food processor (or grind the ground chicken in a mortar and pestle, then add the remaining ingredients one at a time and in order, grinding well as you go).

Make the STUFFING: Beat the eggs lightly, add the sugar, salt, and soy sauce, then stir in the mushroom and carrot. Place the mixture in a double boiler and heat gently, stirring constantly, until it stiffens slightly—it will still be sticky but you should be able to shape it with your hands.

Lay out a length of plastic wrap. Using a spatula or dinner knife, spread a portion of the wrapping into a rectangle ¼ × 3 × 6 inches (½ × 8 × 15 cm). Lay a row of stuffing down the center of the wrapping, and bring up the edges to meet over the stuffing. Press into a neat roll and tie the ends of the plastic with kitchen string. Use a toothpick to prick several small holes in the plastic wrap. Make 2–3 more rolls.

Steam the rolls over medium heat for 15 minutes, cool, and unwrap.

Combine all the SIMMERING ingredients in a large frying pan and bring to a boil over high heat. Add the rolls and simmer, rotating them occasionally so flavor is absorbed evenly and rolls are well coated. Continue cooking until the liquid is almost completely reduced, remove from heat, and sprinkle with ground *sansho* pepper.

Cut the rolls into ½-inch (1-cm) rounds, arrange cut side up, and serve.

47 Cals

Sautéed Duck Breast with Sauce

Aigamo-rosu teriyaki

Success here hinges on the initial pan-frying of the duck: the outside should be quickly fried to a golden brown but the center should still be red. Piercing and weighting the breast removes unwanted fluids and characteristic odors, and a final coating in thickened simmering liquid ensures the richness of this dish.

Serves 15–20

2 duck breasts, ½ lb (220 g) each
1 Tbsp vegetable oil
moutarde de Meaux mustard

FOR SIMMERING
⅔ cup (160 ml) saké
4 Tbsps dark soy sauce
2½ Tbsps *mirin*
2½ Tbsps sugar

Remove the excess skin and fat from the duck breasts.

Heat the oil in a frying pan over high heat, place the duck in skin side down, and fry until golden brown. Turn and fry the other side just briefly until the color of the flesh changes.

Remove the duck, plunge into ample boiling water, and drain.

Combine the SIMMERING ingredients in a saucepan and bring to a boil over high heat. Add the duck, again skin side down, reduce the heat to medium, and simmer for 3 minutes while gently basting.

Remove the duck, pierce each breast in numerous places with a fork, place between 2 plates, and weight with a heavy (1-lb/450-g) object. Let stand for 15 minutes to press out any excess fluid.

Reheat the simmering liquid over a low heat until it forms small bubbles and begins to thicken, then add the duck and coat evenly with sauce.

Remove, slice the duck thinly (⅛ inch/ ⅓ cm), and serve. Season with mustard to taste.

112 Cals

Steamed Abalone

Mushi awabi

Slices of slowly steamed abalone are topped with tiny, tender sea urchin and accented with green peppercorns, glazed with savory gelatin, and finally garnished with fresh mint leaves. Using sheet rather than powdered gelatin gives the sauce better clarity and flavor.

Makes 20 pieces

2 12-oz (360-g) abalone steaks (see Note)

saké

10 oz (300 g) sea urchin

cornstarch

2 Tbsps bottled or canned green peppercorns in brine

small mint leaves or fresh thyme

SAUCE

½ oz (15 g) sheet gelatin or 2 Tbsps gelatin granules

2 cups (480 ml) bonito stock (*dashi*) (page 140)

2½ Tbsps dark soy sauce

1 Tbsp saké

1 Tbsp *mirin*

⅓ tsp salt

Soak the sheet gelatin in water to soften (or soak the powdered gelatin in ½ cup [120 ml] water).

Sprinkle the abalone heavily with salt and scrub well with a brush (a clean toothbrush will do). Wash under running water. Put the abalone in a heatproof casserole or pan, sprinkle with saké, and steam over high heat for 2–2½ hours to tenderize. Cool.

Sprinkle some saké and salt on the sea urchin, then coat lightly with cornstarch. Steam for 3 minutes over high heat, then let cool.

Combine all the SAUCE ingredients, except the gelatin, in a saucepan and bring to a boil over high heat. Remove from heat. Squeeze any excess water from the softened sheet gelatin, then add the gelatin to the sauce. Stir to dissolve the gelatin and pour the mixture through a fine sieve into a bowl. Set the bowl in cold water and force-cool the sauce, stirring constantly.

Cut the abalone into ¼-inch (½-cm) slices and score one side of each slice in a diamond pattern. Arrange the slices on a cake rack, and top with sea urchin and green peppercorns. Pour the sauce over the abalone and

Pour sauce over abalone, sea urchin, and peppercorn

sea urchin and allow it to set for a few minutes. Repeat twice.

Remove the abalone and sea urchin to serving plates, stir through the gelatin once or twice, and spoon it around the abalone and sea urchin. Garnish with mint leaves and serve.

41 Cals

NOTE: If your abalone steaks are 1½ lbs (700 g) or larger, scrub with salt, cut into ¼-inch (½-cm) slices, and beat with a rolling pin to tenderize. Sprinkle the flesh with saké and steam for 1½–2 hours. Cool and cut into 1½-inch (3-cm) squares. Arrange the squares on a cake rack and proceed as above.

Jellied Shrimp and Sea Urchin

Ebi to uni no nikogori

Just the hors d'oeuvre for a cool summer evening. At the ideal consistency (best achieved with the sheet gelatin), the jellied concoction should "melt in the mouth." Many different ingredients can be substituted to vary the effect of this colorful medley—white-fleshed fish or chicken, caviar, asparagus, or other favorites. Served unmolded or chilled in individual glasses, this elegant dish is sure to please.

Serves 20

10 raw shrimp, 1 oz (30 g) each
½ lb (220 g) fresh sea urchin
cornstarch
40 fresh green soybeans in pods or 40 green peas

JELLY

1 oz (30 g) sheet gelatin or 4 Tbsps gelatin granules
1 qt (1 L) bonito stock (*dashi*) (page 140)
⅓ cup (80 ml) dark soy sauce
2 Tbsps saké
2 Tbsps *mirin*
1 tsp salt

10 bamboo skewers

Soften the gelatin in water (or soak the gelatin granules in 1 cup [240 ml] water).

Devein the shrimp (page 48). Thread each shrimp on the underside from head to tail with a bamboo skewer. Boil in lightly salted water for 3 minutes, then drop in cold water and cool. Drain, pull out skewers, shell, and remove head and tail. Cut the shrimp into 1-inch (2½-cm) pieces.

Coat the sea urchin with cornstarch and steam for 5 minutes. If they are very large, cut them in half after steaming.

Boil the soybeans (or green peas), still in their pods, in lightly salted water for 6–7 minutes. Refresh in cold water, drain well, shell, and peel off membrane.

Combine all the JELLY ingredients, except the gelatin, in a saucepan and bring to a boil over high heat. Remove from heat. Squeeze as much water from the softened sheet gelatin as possible. Add the gelatin to the hot mixture and stir gently to dissolve.

Add the shrimp, steamed sea urchin, and soybeans (or peas). Pour into a dampened mold and refrigerate until firm (about 1 hour).

Immerse the mold in hot water to loosen the jelly and turn out onto a plate. Cut into 20 rough blocks. Trim away excess jelly so that a few morsels are nicely framed in each square. Crumble trimmings. Transfer the squares to serving plates and add crumbled jelly around squares.

41 Cals

NOTE: As an alternative, divide the still warm mixture among small tartlet pans or long-stemmed champagne or cocktail glasses to make individual servings.

Grilled Squid with Golden Topping and Oil-Grilled Green Peppers

Ika no kimi-yaki, aoto oiru-yaki

This colorful and fun-to-make appetizer features grilled white squid topped with a bright egg sauce. Take care not to overcook the squid—it should remain moist and tender.

Serves 15–20

1¼ lbs (550 g) squid, cleaned and skinned (page 141)
40 small sweet green peppers or 5 medium bell peppers
vegetable oil

TOPPING

3 egg yolks
dash *mirin*
pinch salt

long metal skewers

Score the squid to half its thickness in a fine diamond pattern on the outside.

Combine the TOPPING ingredients and mix well.

Skewer the squid on the unscored side as shown in Squid Teriyaki (page 44). Sprinkle lightly with salt.

Grill the squid over high heat starting with the scored side. When it whitens, turn and grill the other side. When the second side turns white, brush the topping on the scored side, reduce heat to medium-low, and dry topping. Brush on topping 1 or 2 times more and dry. Do not overcook squid.

Trim the sweet green peppers (or core and seed bell peppers and cut each into 8 strips). Skewer the pepper, brush with vegetable oil, sprinkle lightly with salt, and grill over high heat until just tender.

Remove all the skewers, cut the squid into bite-sized pieces, and arrange on a serving platter with the peppers.

40 Cals

Shimeji Mushrooms with Pine Needles

Shimeji matsuba-zashi

Shimeji mushrooms, prized in Japan for their flavor and texture, are simmered briefly, then skewered on green pine needles—a unique touch for the Western table.

Serves 15–20

14 oz (400 g) *shimeji* or small oyster mushrooms or 4 oz (120 g) dried morels

FOR SIMMERING

1⅔ cups (400 ml) bonito stock (*dashi*) (page 140)
3⅓ Tbsps light soy sauce
3⅓ Tbsps *mirin*
1 Tbsp sugar

stiff pine needles or cocktail toothpicks

Cut off and discard the root portion of the *shimeji* or oyster cluster, separate mush-

rooms, and wash in ample lukewarm water. (If using dried morels, soak in water for 20 minutes to soften, wash under running water to remove the sand, and parboil for 2–3 minutes.)

Combine the SIMMERING ingredients in a saucepan and bring to a boil over high heat. Add the mushrooms and boil for 2 minutes. Remove from heat and set aside for 2 hours to allow the mushrooms to absorb the full flavor.

Drain and skewer the mushrooms on firm, clean pine needles (or cocktail toothpicks).

5 Cals

Shrimp and Sardine Rafts

Ikada-age

Shrimp and sardines riding deep-fried "rafts" of bread are among the more original East-West fare. The frying oil should not be too hot, or else the bread will completely brown before the seafood is heated through. While shrimp and small fish are perhaps more attractive, crab leg, scallops, mussels, and clams might also enjoy a raft voyage.

Makes 40 rafts

vegetable oil for deep-frying
16–20 slices white bread, ½-inch (1½-cm) thick
20 raw shrimp, 1 oz (25 g) each, shelled and deveined (page 48)
20 small sardines, ½ oz (15 g) each
egg whites, lightly beaten
flour
20 lemon wedges

Preheat the oil to a medium deep-frying temperature (340° F/170° C).

Remove the crusts from the bread and cut each slice into ½ × ½ × 3-inch (1½ × 1½ × 8-cm) strips.

Slit open the shrimp along the back side and spread open.

Cut the heads off of the sardines, then make a diagonal cut along the abdomen and remove the intestines (page 36). Wash thoroughly and pat dry.

Dip one side of a bread strip in the egg white and stick it to a second piece so they are slightly out of alignment. Dust the opening on the back of a shrimp with flour, then dip in egg white and stick to the bread raft belly up. Make another raft and attach a sardine, stomach down, in the same way. Make remaining rafts.

Deep-fry the rafts until bread is golden brown (about 2 minutes). Sprinkle with salt while still hot.

Arrange a shrimp raft and a sardine raft on each plate, add a lemon wedge, and serve.

92 Cals

Stick 2 strips of bread together with egg white to make rafts

17

Endive Boats with Avocado, Crab, and Salmon Roe

Andibu no abokado, kani, ikura nose

This dish was inspired by the American-born "California Roll" sushi. Avocado and crab-meat are tossed with a mayonnaise-like sauce and loaded onto endive "boats," then the whole is garnished with sparkling salmon roe. East meets West meets East!

Makes 30–40 boats

2 oz (60 g) salmon roe

7 Tbsps saké

2 medium, ripe avocados

½ lb (220 g) canned crabmeat

2 large heads Belgian endive, about ½ lb (220 g) each

chervil

GOLDEN SAUCE

3 egg yolks

4 Tbsps bonito stock (*dashi*) (page 140)

4 tsps rice vinegar

1 Tbsp *mirin*

1 Tbsp sugar

1 tsp light soy sauce

pinch salt

Soak the salmon roe in the saké for 10 minutes to remove some of the saltiness, then drain.

Cut the avocado in half lengthwise, then pit, peel, and cut into ¼-inch (½-cm) cubes.

Pick through the crab to remove any cartilage and shell.

Separate the endive leaves and cut cross-wise into bite-sized lengths.

Combine the GOLDEN SAUCE ingredients in a double boiler, stirring constantly, until the sauce approaches the consistency of a thin mayonnaise. Force through a fine drum sieve and cool.

Combine the avocado, crab, and sauce and mix gently. Spoon a manageable amount of the mixture on each piece of endive, garnish with the salmon roe and chervil, and serve.

40 Cals

Squid and Asparagus with Mustard-Miso Sauce

Ika asuparagasu karashi-su-miso-ae

Thin spears of squid and asparagus tossed in a Mustard-Miso Sauce and conveniently served in individual cocottes or on the half-shell are hard to resist.

Makes 15–20 petit portions

5 oz (150 g) squid, cleaned and skinned (page 141)
dash saké
6 stalks green asparagus, trimmed
dash light soy sauce

MUSTARD-MISO SAUCE

1 egg yolk
5 Tbsps nonsweet white miso paste

3 Tbsps sugar
2½ Tbsps rice vinegar
2 Tbsps bonito stock (*dashi*) (page 140)
1½ tsps hot yellow mustard (*karashi*) or any mustard that is not sweet or vinegary
1 tsp light soy sauce

Combine all the MUSTARD-MISO SAUCE ingredients in a double boiler and heat gradually, stirring until the sauce reaches the consistency of a mayonnaise. Cool.

Cut the squid into ⅛ × ⅛ × 1-inch (⅓ × ⅓ × 3-cm) strips. Combine the saké and a pinch salt in a saucepan over high heat, add the squid, and cook until it turns white. Drain and cool.

Cut the asparagus to the same size as the squid, boil until just tender in lightly salted water, refresh in cold water, and drain. Sprinkle with the soy sauce and drain again.

Combine the squid and asparagus, toss well with the sauce, and arrange in serving dishes.

32 Cals

Jade Green Deep-Fried Shrimp

Ebi hisui-age

Shrimp deep-fried with thinly sliced ginkgo nuts need only a pinch of salt for seasoning. The colors are something to be relished—the ginkgo nuts turn jade green and make an appetizing contrast to the pink of the shrimp. Watch these precious jewels disappear!

Makes 20 pieces

60 ginkgo nuts
vegetable oil for deep-frying
20 raw shrimp, ⅔ oz (20 g) each
flour
egg white

Shell the ginkgo nuts (page 141) and use your fingers to remove the inner brown skin, without blanching. Slice the nuts as thinly as possible.

Preheat the oil to a medium deep-frying temperature (340° F/170° C).

Shell and devein the shrimp (page 48), leaving the tails intact.

Dip the shrimp first in flour, then in egg white, and finally in the thinly sliced ginkgo nuts.

Deep-fry shrimp for 2 minutes. Sprinkle with salt and serve.

50 Cals

Soups

Crab Ball Soup

Kani-iri-shinjo no suimono

Balls of ground fish or shellfish, steamed or boiled, are considered to be the ultimate ingredient for clear soups. Extremely delicate, they should be steamed or simmered slowly over low heat or they will lose their fine texture. Once they have been cooked, they can also be deep-fried or added to other simmered dishes. Here crab was used, so a light-flavored white fish was chosen as the basic ingredient, but there are any number of variations. Try replacing the crab-and-fish combination with either scallops or shrimp.

Serves 4

1-inch (2½-cm) piece fresh ginger (½ oz/ 15 g)

1½ oz (50 g) green beans (about 12)

4 fresh shiitake mushrooms, washed and stems removed, or 4 fresh brown mushrooms, washed and trimmed

¼ medium carrot

4 bunches corn salad, about 7 oz (200 g) total

2½ cups (600 ml) bonito stock (*dashi*) (page 140)

⅓ tsp salt

1 tsp light soy sauce

2 Tbsps cornstarch dissolved in 2 Tbsps water

CRAB BALLS

1 dried cloud ear mushroom

3½ oz (100 g) frozen crabmeat, shredded

14 oz (400 g) flounder, turbot, or any firm white-fleshed fish fillets

2 egg whites

2 Tbsps cornstarch dissolved in 2 Tbsps water

dash saké

pinch salt

dash *mirin*

TO PREPARE

Soak the cloud ear for 1 hour (page 142). Cut into fine slivers, parboil, refresh in cold water, and drain.

Steam the crab for 5 minutes over high heat. Cool and drain. Check for cartilage or pieces of shell.

Cut the ginger with the grain into extremely fine slivers, soak in water for 2–3 minutes, and drain.

TO MAKE

Parboil the green beans and shiitake (or brown) mushrooms separately in lightly salted water. Refresh in cold water and drain. Cut the green beans into long ⅛-inch (¼-cm) thick strips.

Cut the carrot into strips the same size as the green beans, parboil in lightly salted water, refresh in cold water, and drain.

Blanch the corn salad in lightly salted boiling water, refresh in cold water, and drain.

Place the bonito stock in a soup pot, add the salt, and bring to a boil over high heat. Add the soy sauce and remove from heat.

Divide 1 cup (240 ml) of the bonito stock among 4 small bowls and soak the shiitake (or brown) mushrooms, green beans, carrot, and corn salad separately.

Make the CRAB BALLS: Whir the fish in a food processor, add the egg whites, cornstarch dissolved in water, saké, salt, and *mirin*, and whir to a smooth paste. Transfer to a bowl, add the crab and cloud ear, and mix well. Set a pot of water to boil, then adjust the heat so the water remains just below the boiling point. Divide the crab mixture into 4 equal portions and form each into a large ball. Wrap each ball in plastic wrap and tie with kitchen string. Place the balls in the hot water and cook 7–8 minutes, adjusting heat so water remains just below the boiling point. Drain, unwrap, and arrange in bowls.

Warm the mushrooms, green beans, carrot, and corn salad in their soaking liquid. Place a bit of each vegetable in the soup bowls, reserving the soaking liquid.

Combine the bonito stock from the vegetables and the remaining 1½ cups (360 ml) stock in a saucepan and bring to a boil over high heat. When it boils, thicken with the

cornstarch dissolved in water. Return to a boil, then divide the hot broth among the bowls. Top with the ginger slivers and serve.
158 Cals

Combine whirred ingredients with crab and cloud ear mushroom

Cook wrapped crab balls for 7–8 minutes

Clam Soup

Hamaguri ushio-jiru

Shellfish are so flavorful that a little season-
ing is all that is needed to make a rich broth.
When the shells barely crack open, the clams
are done and should be served immediately.
In cold weather, the soup can be thickened
slightly with starch to retain heat longer.

Serves 4

12 live hard-shell clams, 2 oz (60 g) each

⅓ oz (10 g) dried *wakame* seaweed

1 bunch *enoki* mushrooms or 4 oz (120 g)
   oyster mushrooms

1½ cups (360 ml) water

1½ cups (360 ml) bonito stock (*dashi*)
   (page 140)

2-inch (5-cm) length kelp (*konbu*)

pinch salt

dash light soy sauce

dash saké

2-inch (5-cm) piece fresh ginger, finely
   slivered (1 oz/30 g)

TO PREPARE

Choose fresh clams that close tightly when
they are touched. Avoid ones with cracked
or chipped shells.

Let the clams stand in salted water (1 tsp
salt to 3 cups [700 ml] water) in a cool, dark
place for 5–6 hours to allow them to expel
sand.

Prepare the *wakame* seaweed (page 143).
Chop into 1½-inch (4-cm) lengths.

Cut away the root cluster at the base of
the *enoki* mushrooms (or trim oyster mushrooms). Parboil in lightly salted water, then
plunge into cold water. Drain.

TO MAKE

Combine the clams, water, bonito stock, and
konbu kelp in a soup pot over high heat. Just
before the water boils, remove the kelp.
Bring the water to a boil. When the clams
open, remove them from the pot and discard
any that do not open. Strain the broth to
clarify (page 142).

Return the broth to the pot and season to
taste with salt, soy sauce, and saké. Reheat
the mushrooms and *wakame* seaweed in the
broth.

Divide the clams, mushrooms, and *wakame* seaweed among 4 bowls. Add the
broth, top with the slivered ginger root, and
serve.

114 Cals

Chicken Ball and Cucumber Soup

Tori-gan kyuri supu-jitate

This simple, hearty soup, using familiar ingre-
dients, exploits the fresh lightness of cucum-
ber and the zesty flavor of ginger. Turnip,
daikon radish, or eggplant are excellent alter-
natives to the cucumber. This dish can substi-
tute for a simmered dish if the volume of soup
is reduced and a small amount of cornstarch
is added to thicken it.

Serves 4

1 cucumber

1 Tbsp saké

2 tsps light soy sauce

⅓ tsp salt

1 tsp fresh ginger juice (page 145)

STOCK

bones from one chicken

3 qts (3 L) water

2-inch (5-cm) length kelp (*konbu*)

CHICKEN BALLS

7 oz (200 g) ground chicken
1 egg, lightly beaten
3 Tbsps cornstarch
dash saké
dash *mirin*
dash dark soy sauce
dash fresh ginger juice (page 145)

TO PREPARE

Make the STOCK: Place the chicken bones in a bowl and cover with boiling water. When the remaining flesh turns white, remove the bones, wash under cold running water, and drain. Break up the bones into large pieces and place in a soup pot. Add the water and kelp, place over high heat, and bring to a boil, removing the kelp just before the water boils. Reduce heat to low and simmer, skimming occasionally, until the stock is reduced to a third of the original volume. Strain the finished stock to clarify (page 142).

TO MAKE

Peel the cucumber, slice in half lengthwise, and scrape out the seeds with a spoon. Slice the halves into 1-inch (2½-cm) lengths. Par-boil the cucumber in lightly salted water, drain, refresh in cold water, and drain again.

Combine all the CHICKEN BALL ingredients in a food processor and whir to a fine paste (or place the chicken in a mortar and pestle, grind, then add the remaining ingredients in order and one at a time, grinding after each addition).

Bring 3 cups (700 ml) chicken stock to a boil in a soup pot over high heat. Form the chicken mixture into balls about 1 inch (2½ cm) in diameter and drop in the boiling stock. When they return to the surface, boil 2–3 minutes. Remove the chicken balls and drain. Strain the soup to clarify.

Return the stock to the pot and place over high heat. Season with the saké, soy sauce, and salt. Add the chicken balls and cucumber and boil for 2–3 minutes. Add the ginger juice and remove from heat. Transfer to soup bowls and serve.

168 Cals

Add enough boiling water to cover bones

Bring bones and kelp to a boil over high heat, removing kelp just before water boils

Tofu, Pork, and Vegetable Soup

Kenchin jiru

This recipe seems to have its origins in traditional Chinese cuisine. The vegetables are stir-fried in order to reduce their moisture and bring out their characteristic tastes. Chicken, duck, or fish (especially cod) can be substituted for pork, and almost any vegetable can be used. Chicken stock will serve very well for bonito stock, and a little cornstarch at the end will not only thicken the soup, but also keep it hot longer.

Serves 4

4 oz (120 g) *konnyaku*
2 oz (60 g) watercress or spinach
5 oz (150 g) boneless pork loin
2 oz (60 g) canned bamboo shoots
½ medium carrot
1 fresh shiitake mushroom, washed and stem removed, or 1 fresh brown mushroom, washed and trimmed
1 block regular ("cotton") tofu, about 10 oz (300 g)
2 Tbsps vegetable oil
3⅓ cups (800 ml) bonito stock (*dashi*) (page 140)
2 tsps light soy sauce
⅓ tsp salt
3 Tbsps cornstarch dissolved in 3 Tbsps water
1 Tbsp fresh ginger juice (page 145)

Cut the *konnyaku* into ⅛ × ¼ × 1-inch (¼ × ½ × 3-cm) strips. Rub with salt, then boil for about 5 minutes and drain (page 142).

Cook the watercress (or the spinach) in lightly salted boiling water until just tender, then immediately refresh in cold water. Drain, wring out excess water, and cut into 1½-inch (4-cm) lengths.

Slice the pork loin into ¼ × ¼ × 2-inch (½ × ½ × 5-cm) strips.

Wash and prepare the bamboo shoots (see Miso Soup on facing page).

Cut the bamboo shoots into 2-inch (5-cm) long julienne strips. Sliver the carrot. Slice the mushroom cap thinly.

Crumble the tofu coarsely by hand.

Heat the oil in a soup pot over medium heat, then add the pork and sauté until it turns white. Add the tofu and stir-fry until the excess water is cooked off (about 3 minutes).

Stir in the carrot, bamboo shoot, mushroom, and *konnyaku*. Continue to stir-fry over medium heat until the vegetables are just tender, then add the stock.

When the soup boils, adjust the seasoning with the soy sauce and salt. Return to a boil and thicken with the cornstarch dissolved in water. Boil again, add the watercress (or spinach) and ginger juice, remove from heat, and transfer to soup bowls.

274 Cals

Pureed Corn Soup

Tomorokoshi suri-nagashi

As do their Western counterparts, Japanese cooks often blend pureed vegetables or seafood—scallops, shrimp, crab, and white-fleshed fish—into broth to make rich soups. This is one such soup, a Japanese-style corn soup. Meat, fish, and shellfish make welcome accents to vegetable soups prepared in this way, just as vegetables harmonize beautifully with seafood soups. Try your hand at different flavor combinations.

Serves 4

2 oz (60 g) boned chicken breast
2 pods okra
1⅔ cups (400 ml) bonito stock (*dashi*) (page 140)
¼ tsp salt
1 tsp light soy sauce
2 Tbsps nonsweet white miso paste
1½ cups (200 g) corn kernels (about 2 ears)

Dice the chicken, boil in lightly salted water until done, then refresh in cold water and drain.

Rub the okra with salt, using a scrubbing motion to remove the tiny hairs from the outside of the pods. Drop the okra in lightly salted boiling water, cook until just tender, refresh in cold water, and drain. Cut the pods into thin rounds.

Heat the bonito stock in a soup pot over high heat, add the salt, and bring to a boil. Add the soy sauce. Remove ½ cup (120 ml) of the hot soup and thin the miso paste. Add the thinned miso to the soup, mix well, and remove from heat.

Cook the corn in lightly salted water. Drain well. Combine the corn and soup in a food processor or blender, whir thoroughly, and then force through a fine sieve.

Return the corn mixture to the soup pot and add the chicken. Bring to a boil over high heat. Transfer to soup bowls, float the okra rounds on top, and serve.

150 Cals

Miso Soup with Pork and Vegetables

Buta jiru

Miso soup, that most Japanese of soups, is extremely congenial to fatty meats, and the addition of pork in particular gives it a fuller body and flavor. The vegetables have been selected with an eye toward color, texture, and flavor, and the seven-spice pepper adds a final flourish.

Serves 4

6 oz (180 g) boneless pork loin

2 oz (60 g) canned bamboo shoots

2 stalks green asparagus, trimmed

½ medium carrot

4 fresh shiitake mushrooms, washed and stems removed, or 4 fresh brown mushrooms, washed and trimmed

2 scallions

2 Tbsps vegetable oil

3⅓ cups (800 ml) bonito stock (*dashi*) (page 140)

6 Tbsps nonsweet white miso paste

seven-spice pepper (*shichimi*), cayenne pepper, or pepper

Slice the pork as thinly as possible and cut into ½ × 1-inch (1 × 3-cm) strips.

Wash the bamboo well and scrub away any white residue. Add an ample amount of water and the bamboo shoots to a saucepan and bring to a boil over high heat. Reduce the heat to medium and boil for 5 minutes. Refresh in cold water. Cool and drain.

Cut the asparagus, bamboo shoots, and carrot into 1½-inch (4-cm) long julienne strips. Slice the mushroom caps thinly. Sliver the scallions diagonally.

Heat the oil in a saucepan over high heat. Add the pork and stir-fry briefly until it turns white. Add the carrot, bamboo shoot, mushroom, and asparagus and continue stir-frying until the vegetables are just tender. Add the bonito stock and heat to a boil. Reduce heat to low and simmer for 10 minutes, skimming occasionally.

While the soup is simmering, place the miso in a bowl and thin with ½ cup (120 ml) of the hot broth. Add the miso to the soup, adjust the seasoning, bring to a boil, add the scallion, then immediately remove from heat.

Divide the soup among 4 bowls and sprinkle with pepper before serving.

263 Cals

Scallop and Vegetable Soup

Kai-bashira no sawani-jiru

A truly hearty soup full of tasty, bite-sized tidbits. The delicate scallops need only a minimum of cooking, and should be added at the very last along with the snow peas, which lose their color if introduced too soon. Substitute shrimp, crab, oysters, or clams for the scallops.

Serves 4

3 shucked scallops, about 2 oz (60 g) each

1½ oz (50 g) snow peas (about 20)

½ medium carrot

4 fresh shiitake mushrooms, washed and stems removed, or 4 fresh brown mushrooms, washed and trimmed

1 qt (1 L) chicken stock (page 22)

1½ tsps light soy sauce

1 tsp saké

1 tsp salt

pepper

If the scallops are uncleaned, remove the surrounding membrane and the tough white ligament (page 133). Cut the scallops into strips of approximately ¼ × ¼ × 1½ inches (½ × ½ × 4 cm).

String the snow peas. Cut the carrot and snow peas into 1½-inch (4-cm) long fine slivers. Cut the mushroom caps into thin slices.

Place the chicken stock in a soup pot, bring to a boil over high heat, and add the carrot and mushroom. When the vegetables are just tender, add the soy sauce, saké, salt, and pepper to taste. Add the snow peas and scallops, cook for 1 minute longer, and transfer to soup bowls.

47 Cals

Fish

Quick-Seared Bonito Sashimi
Katsuo tataki-zukuri

The name tataki implies a beating in of the flavor and was originally quite literal. Fillets singed over a high flame were sprinkled with condiments, the flavors of which were then lightly patted into the fish with the broad side of a knife. Other strong condiments such as hot yellow mustard (karashi) and garlic go well with tataki. For a related recipe, see Beef Tartare, Japanese Style (page 52).

Serves 4

1 lb (450 g) very fresh bonito, tuna, or
   Spanish mackerel fillets, with skin
juice from 1 lemon

LEMON-SOY DIPPING SAUCE (*Ponzu*)

7 Tbsps lemon juice
7 Tbsps dark soy sauce
5 Tbsps rice vinegar
5 tsps *mirin*, alcohol burned off (page 146)
1 Tbsp tamari soy sauce (see Note, page 51)
¼ cup loose bonito flakes (⅙ oz/5 g)
1-inch (2½-cm) length kelp (*konbu*)

CONDIMENTS

20 *shiso*, basil, or mint leaves
1 head Belgian endive, about 7 oz (200 g)
4 Tbsps finely chopped fresh ginger
4 Tbsps finely chopped and rinsed scallion
2 Tbsps Red Maple Radish (page 140)

long metal skewers

TO PREPARE

Combine all the LEMON-SOY DIPPING SAUCE
ingredients, mix well, and refrigerate for 24
hours to allow flavor to fully mature. Strain
to clarify (page 142).

Remove the stalks and any tough veins
from the *shiso* (or basil or mint) leaves and
cut into very fine slivers. Submerge the
slivers in cold water for a few seconds, then
drain.

Cut the endive into 1-inch (3-cm) long
julienne strips.

TO MAKE

Cut away any dark, blood-colored sections
of the fillet. Insert the skewers so that they
fan out into and support all parts of the fillet,
and the blunt ends can be gripped with one
hand. Sprinkle the fish lightly with salt.

Briefly grill the fish over a very hot gas
flame on all sides. Grill the skin side first until
it scorches, moving the fish as necessary to
facilitate even grilling. Turn and grill the flesh
side(s) until the surface turns white. Immediately remove from heat and plunge into ice
water.

Carefully remove the skewers in a slow,
twisting motion. When the fish cools, drain
and pat dry.

Place the fish on a cutting board, skin side
up, with the thicker flesh away from you.
Work from the right side of the fish, cutting
½-inch (1-cm) thick slices.

Sprinkle the slices with lemon juice, wrap
in plastic wrap, and refrigerate for 1 hour.

Combine the ginger, *shiso* (or basil or
mint) leaves, and scallion.

Arrange the fish neatly on a clean surface.
Pat on the ginger-*shiso*-scallion mixture.
Remove the fish slices to serving dishes and
garnish with endive and Red Maple Radish.
Serve each diner a bowl of Lemon-Soy Dip-
ping Sauce to be seasoned with the radish.

191 Cals

Tuna Sashimi with Grated Radish

Maguro oroshi-zukuri

Deep red tuna cut into bite-sized cubes and garnished with fresh condiments is as inviting to the eye as it is refreshing to the palate. Bonito, yellowtail, and other fish with tender oily flesh can also be prepared in this way. Be sure to choose very fresh, sashimi-quality fish and if in doubt consult your fishmonger.

Serves 4

1 lb (450 g) very fresh tuna fillet

TOSA DIPPING SAUCE

½ cup (120 ml) dark soy sauce

1 Tbsp saké

1 Tbsp *mirin*

2 Tbsps tamari soy sauce (or substitute an additional 2 Tbsps dark soy sauce)

¼ cup loose bonito flakes (⅙ oz/5 g)

CONDIMENTS

1 sheet *nori* seaweed

8-inch (20-cm) piece daikon radish, finely grated (or substitute peeled, seeded, and grated cucumber)

2–3 Tbsps chopped and rinsed scallion

wasabi horseradish

TO PREPARE

Make the TOSA DIPPING SAUCE: Combine the dark soy sauce, saké, and *mirin* in a saucepan. Bring to a boil over high heat, reduce heat to low, simmer until the volume is reduced slightly (about 10 percent), remove from heat, and add the tamari soy sauce and bonito flakes. Let stand for 5–6 hours. Strain to clarify (page 142). (Tightly sealed in a jar, Tosa Dipping Sauce can be stored for up to 3 months at room temperature.)

Toast the *nori* seaweed over a high gas flame (if it has not been pretoasted), then crumble (page 143).

TO MAKE

Slice the tuna into ¾-inch (2-cm) cubes and stack in serving bowls.

Gently squeeze some (but not all) of the excess moisture from the grated daikon radish with your fingers. Combine the daikon radish, scallion, and *nori* seaweed and mix well. Stack mixture in dish. Carefully pour 1–1½ Tbsps of the Tosa Dipping Sauce around the tuna, add a mound of *wasabi* horseradish, and serve.

408 Cals

Paper-Thin Sea Bass Sashimi

Suzuki usu-zukuri

"Paper-thin" is not an exaggeration; the best chefs can wield a sashimi knife to cut slices so thin the designs on the serving plate show through. Many firm-fleshed varieties of fish are used for this style of sashimi. Ask your fishmonger for sashimi-quality fish. Choose only the freshest ones—those with shiny, clear eyes, firm bellies, and a fresh ocean aroma. Here Tosa Dipping Sauce is used, but Lemon-Soy Dipping Sauce (page 50) works just as well.

Serves 4

1 lb (450 g) sea bass, flounder, or red snapper fillets

TOSA DIPPING SAUCE

½ cup (120 ml) dark soy sauce

1 Tbsp saké

1 Tbsp *mirin*

2 Tbsps tamari soy sauce (or increase the dark soy sauce by 2 Tbsps)

¼ cup loose bonito flakes (⅙ oz/5 g)

CONDIMENTS

½ cucumber

4 mint leaves

wasabi horseradish

4 lemon wedges

TO PREPARE

For best results, prepare the TOSA DIPPING SAUCE (see opposite page) 5–6 hours before serving the sashimi.

TO MAKE

Prepare the CONDIMENTS: Peel the cucumber, seed, and cut into 1½-inch (4-cm) julienne strips. Place in cold water for a moment, then drain.

Place the fillet on a cutting board, skin side up, with the thicker part of the flesh away from you. Work from the left of the fillet, slicing with the entire blade of the knife. Hold the blade as shown and cut away very thin slices by pulling the knife toward you.

After you cut each slice, arrange it on the serving plate. Garnish with the julienned cucumber, mint leaves, *wasabi* horseradish, and lemon wedges. Serve with bowls of Tosa Dipping Sauce.

142 Cals

Slice the fish as thinly as possible

Night-Dried Sole

Shitabirame ichiya-boshi

This curiously named preparation is actually lightly salted and then dried overnight to concentrate the flavor. Brushing on ginger juice, lemon juice, or soy sauce instead of the glaze makes for pleasant taste variations. A natural accompaniment to saké and other drinks, Night-Dried Sole lends itself equally well to other treatments. Deep-fry it, or combine grilled strips with vegetables, then toss in a vinaigrette sauce or a topping such as Mustard-Miso Sauce (page 19).

Serves 4

1⅓ lbs (600 g) sole, halibut, turbot, or flounder fillets, ⅓ inch (¾ cm) thick or less

2-inch (5-cm) length kelp (*konbu*)

4 lemon wedges

GLAZE

1 Tbsp saké

1 Tbsp *mirin*

8 long metal skewers

TO PREPARE

Place the fish and kelp in ample salted water (4 tsps salt to 3 cups [700 ml] water) and let fillets soak for 1 hour.

Drain, then skewer the fillets crosswise through the broader end. Hang the fish in a cool, dark place overnight to dry.

After drying, the surface of the fish should be slightly sticky to the touch. Remove the skewers.

TO MAKE

Grill both sides of the fish on a wire rack over a hot gas flame (about 1½ minutes per side). Combine the saké and *mirin*, and just before the fish is done, brush on the GLAZE.

Cut the fish into bite-sized pieces and arrange in serving dishes. Serve with lemon wedges.

71 Cals

Thread fillets on long skewer and hang up overnight

Deep-Fried Flounder Boat

Karei kara-age

Along with batter-dipped tempura, flour-coating (kara-age) is one of the most important deep-frying techniques in Japanese cooking. An interesting twist here is that the fillets and bones are each fried in a separate way. The bones are fried at a low temperature until all moisture is removed and they turn a golden brown. Then they are eaten like potato chips, being crisp and subtly nutlike. The filleted nuggets are fried at a slightly higher temperature, and only a very short time, until they are cooked through but still moist and tender. They can be eaten with Lemon-Soy Dipping Sauce, lemon juice, or even tempura dipping sauce. Any small white-fleshed fish can also be prepared in this way.

Serves 4

4 flounder, sole, turbot, or halibut, about ½ lb (220 g) each, filleted with bones reserved (see To Prepare)

vegetable oil for deep-frying

12 small sweet green peppers or 2 bell peppers

flour

⅓ oz (10 g) cellophane noodles (*harusame*)

LEMON-SOY DIPPING SAUCE (*Ponzu*)

7 Tbsps lemon juice

7 Tbsps dark soy sauce

5 Tbsps rice vinegar

5 tsps *mirin*, alcohol burned off (page 146)

1 Tbsp tamari soy sauce (see Note)

¼ cup loose bonito flakes (⅙ oz/5 g)

1-inch (2½-cm) length kelp (*konbu*)

CONDIMENTS

4 Tbsps finely chopped and rinsed scallion

4 Tbsps grated daikon radish or white radish

juice from 1 lemon

salt

TO PREPARE

Combine all the LEMON-SOY DIPPING SAUCE ingredients, mix well, and refrigerate for 24 hours to allow flavor to fully mature. After refrigeration, strain to clarify (page 142).

Fillet the fish (or have the fishmonger do this for you), leaving the skin attached to each fillet. Reserve the bones, with head and tail attached.

TO MAKE

Preheat the oil to a low deep-frying temperature (330° F/165° C).

Trim the small sweet green peppers and slash completely through the flesh once to keep them from bursting during deep-frying. (If using bell peppers, seed and then cut each pepper into 8 strips.)

Cut each fillet into bite-sized pieces. Dredge the pieces and the bones in flour.

Deep-fry the bones slowly, and hold up the head as shown until the curve is set. Finish deep-frying.

When the bones have turned brown and become crisp, remove and raise the oil temperature to a high deep-frying temperature (350° F/175° C) and add the fish. Deep-fry to a golden brown. Drain on absorbent paper.

Deep-fry the peppers for about 1 minute. Be careful not to overcook them.

Use scissors to cut the cellophane noodles into 2-inch (5-cm) lengths. Drop in the oil. They will immediately puff up and turn white. As soon as they do, remove from the oil.

TO SERVE

Line serving plates with absorbent paper. Set the boat on the paper and spread the crisp cellophane noodles alongside the boat. Arrange the fish in the boats and garnish the plate with the pepper.

Dip the fish in sauce flavored with scallion and daikon radish, or in lemon juice seasoned with salt to taste.

515 Cals

NOTE: If you do not have tamari soy sauce for the Lemon-Soy Dipping Sauce, make this quick substitute: Combine 4 parts bonito stock, 1 part *mirin*, and 1 part dark soy sauce. Bring to a boil, add ¼ cup loose bonito flakes, and immediately strain to clarify (page 142). Serve sauce lukewarm.

Fillet fish, leaving skin attached

Deep-fry bones first, holding head up in oil until curve is set

31

Deep-Fried Sea Bass

Suzuki iri-dashi

Sea bass tends to be tough and has a strong smell, so deep-frying it in strips is the perfect solution. The lean flesh on the back or toward the tail is better suited to this approach than the oily flesh of the belly. Here Soy-Bonito Dipping Sauce is used, but lemon juice with salt added to taste makes a fine complement too. Still other variations might include topping with a glaze or thickened broth, adding to a soup, or deep-frying the strips at a low oil temperature until crisp, and serving plain with drinks.

Serves 4

vegetable oil for deep-frying
1 lb (450 g) sea bass, flounder, red snapper, or turbot fillets
flour
12 stalks green asparagus, trimmed

SOY-BONITO DIPPING SAUCE

2 cups (480 ml) bonito stock (*dashi*) (page 140)
½ cup (120 ml) dark soy sauce
½ cup (120 ml) *mirin*
¼ cup loose bonito flakes (⅙ oz/5 g)

Slice fish

Coat with flour

CONDIMENTS

4 Tbsps Red Maple Radish (page 140)
4 Tbsps finely chopped and rinsed scallion

Preheat the oil to a high deep-frying temperature (360° F/180° C).

Slice the fillet diagonally into ½-inch (1-cm) wide strips. Brush with flour.

Deep-fry the fish to a golden brown.

Deep-fry the asparagus until just tender.

Combine all the SOY-BONITO DIPPING SAUCE ingredients, except the bonito flakes, in a saucepan and bring to a boil over high heat. Add the bonito flakes, immediately remove from heat, and strain to clarify (page 142).

Arrange the fish and asparagus on serving plates. Provide individual bowls of the dipping sauce with small mounds of Red Maple Radish and chopped scallion.

377 Cals

Simmered Rockfish

Mebaru nitsuke

Nitsuke simmering is a key technique in the Japanese repertoire of cooking fish. The saké-rich broth removes unwanted fish odors and leaves the flesh succulent, while ideally, brisk heating makes for easy boning. Neither too much nor too little liquid will produce the desired result; choosing the right-sized pot and always using a drop-lid (page 143) will ensure that the liquid circulates. The fish can be served piping hot, or for a different taste, eaten chilled in its jelled broth.

Serves 4

4 rockfish, flounder, turbot, or halibut fillets, 3–4 oz (90–120 g) each
12 oz (360 g) canned bamboo shoots
¼ bunch thyme

FOR SIMMERING

1¼ cups (300 ml) saké
5 Tbsps *mirin*
2½ Tbsps dark soy sauce
2½ Tbsps sugar
1 Tbsp tamari soy sauce (or increase dark
   soy sauce by 1 Tbsp)
1 Tbsp fresh ginger juice (page 145)

Score each side of the fish. Place in a bowl and cover with boiling water. When the skin whitens, immerse in cold water and remove any remaining debris. Wash well. Drain.

Wash bamboo shoots well, scrubbing away any white calcium residue. Combine the bamboo shoots and ample water in a saucepan and bring to a boil over high heat. Reduce heat to medium and simmer for 5 minutes. Drop in cold water to cool, then drain and quarter lengthwise.

Combine the saké, *mirin*, soy sauce, and sugar in a saucepan and bring to a boil over

Cover scored fish with boiling water until skin turns white

high heat. Set the rockfish carefully in the simmering liquid. Cover with a drop-lid and cook for 10 minutes over high heat. Add the bamboo shoots and continue to cook.

When the liquid is reduced by about half, add the tamari soy sauce and ginger juice. Simmer for about 5 more minutes, occasionally ladling sauce over the fish and bamboo

When sauce thickens slightly, remove from heat

shoots. When the sauce begins to thicken slightly, remove from heat.

Arrange the fish and bamboo shoots in serving bowls and add several tablespoons of the sauce. Garnish with thyme.

205 Cals

Yuan-Style Grilled Butterfish

Managatsuo Yuan-yaki

Said to have been the creation of the renowned gourmet Kitamura Yuan, Yuan-style grilling, which requires a lavish amount of saké, yields fish that is tender, free of fish odors, and absolutely delicious hot or cold. A touch of lemon or lime in the marinade adds further piquancy. Pork, chicken, beef, and duck can also be cooked in this manner.

Serves 4

1 lb (450 g) butterfish, sea bass, or yellow-tail fillets, with skin
1 lemon, thinly sliced
2 Tbsps *mirin*

MARINADE

½ cup (120 ml) dark soy sauce
½ cup (120 ml) saké
½ cup (120 ml) *mirin*

long metal skewers (if grilling)

Score pieces at ¼-inch (½-cm) intervals

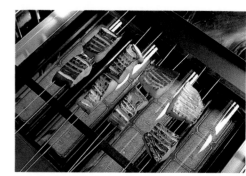

Skewer fish and then grill or broil

TO PREPARE

Sprinkle both sides of the fillets lightly with salt and let stand for 1 hour.

Wash the fish and cut into 8 pieces.

Combine all the MARINADE ingredients and mix well. Add 2–3 slices lemon. Marinate the fish for 30–40 minutes.

TO MAKE

Remove the fish and reserve the marinade. Wipe the fish dry, then score the skin at ¼-inch (½-cm) intervals.

Cook the fish according to one of the following methods.

Grilling: Skewer the fish lengthwise. Grill, skin side first, over a medium-high gas flame.

Remove the fish from the heat and, with a bowl underneath to catch the excess, pour marinade over the fish 2 or 3 times during grilling. Cooking time should be approximately 6–7 minutes; turn once. When the fish is almost done, brush the skin side with *mirin* to glaze.

Broiling: Place the fish, skin side down, on the broiler rack and cook under hot flame 12–13 minutes, brushing occasionally with the marinade. Turn the fish once. Brush on *mirin* to glaze just before fish is done.

Gently twist and then pull out the skewers. Arrange the fish on top of the sliced lemon on serving plates.

236 Cals

Yellowtail Teriyaki

Buri teriyaki

Since cooked yellowtail is soft and extremely delicate, lightly salting the fillets to firm them up beforehand is highly recommended. A lengthy marination yields the most flavor for the least actual cooking time. Finally, whether grilling on skewers or using the fry-pan method, carefully browning the fillets on both sides before pouring on the Teriyaki Sauce seals the juicy insides in a delicious glazed crust. Ginger juice may be added to the sauce as desired to mask odors or for an extra bite.

Serves 4

4 yellowtail fillets, with skin if possible, about ½ lb (220 g) each (or substitute herring)
1 Tbsp vegetable oil (if pan-frying)

TURNIP CHRYSANTHEMUMS

1 medium turnip
2-inch (5-cm) length kelp (*konbu*)
½ cup (120 ml) rice vinegar
½ cup (120 ml) water
4 tsps sugar
pinch salt
2 dried red chili peppers

TERIYAKI SAUCE

1 cup (240 ml) *mirin*
⅔ cup (160 ml) saké
½ cup (120 ml) dark soy sauce
3 Tbsps tamari soy sauce (or increase dark soy sauce and *mirin* by 3 Tbsps each)

12 long metal skewers (if grilling)

TO PREPARE

Begin preparing the TURNIP CHRYSANTHEMUM garnish (page 141) 1½–2 hours before serving time.

Combine all the TERIYAKI SAUCE ingredients, bring to a boil over high heat, reduce heat to low, and simmer until volume is slightly reduced (about 10 percent).

Sprinkle the yellowtail fillets with salt and let stand for 15 minutes. Wash and pat dry. Marinate in the Teriyaki Sauce for 1 hour.

TO MAKE

Remove the fillets from the Teriyaki Sauce and reserve the sauce. Cook the fillets using one of the following methods.

Grilling: Using 3 skewers per fillet, insert so that skewers fan out into fish. Grill over a medium-high gas flame until slightly browned. Turn and grill the other side. Just before the fish is done, momentarily withdraw it from the flame, and holding it over a bowl, pour on an ample amount of the Teriyaki Sauce.

Pan-frying: Heat 1 Tbsp vegetable oil in a skillet over medium-high heat. Add the fillets and fry until golden brown. Turn and fry the other side. When the fish is almost done, add ⅓ cup (80 ml) Teriyaki Sauce and coat well.

Carefully remove the skewers. Cut each fillet into 2 or 3 pieces and arrange on serving plates. Garnish each plate with Turnip Chrysanthemums.

764 Cals

Sardines Simmered with Ginger

Iwashi shoga-ni

Sardines are all too often avoided because of their pungent odor. Three tips for preparing these economical, nutritious, and truly tasty fish make all the difference. First, rinse them over and over again in many changes of water after scaling and cleaning; second, precook them in water and vinegar until tender straight through to the bone, then discard the cloudy liquid; third, season them well and simmer slowly. After simmering, they will keep at peak flavor for 2 to 3 weeks refrigerated in a sealed container. In Japan they are most often enjoyed with drinks, but why not make the best of East and West by trying them on canapés?

Serves 4

40 sardines, about 4–5 inches (10–12 cm) each

3-inch (8-cm) piece fresh ginger (1½ oz/ 45 g)

Scale and gut sardines

Arrange sardines in a circle

FOR SIMMERING

1⅔ cups (400 ml) water
¾ cup (180 ml) rice vinegar
3⅓ cups (800 ml) saké (or water)
1¼ cups (300 ml) *mirin*
2 Tbsps sugar
¾ cup (180 ml) dark soy sauce

TO PREPARE

Wash the sardines in salt water — 5 tsps salt to 1 qt (1 L) water. Use your fingers to remove as many scales as possible. Cut the heads off just behind the gills. There are harder bones in the stomach cavity, so cut away a portion of the abdomen on a diagonal from the head end. Remove the intestines. Cut away half

the tail. Wash the sardines well in ample cold water until it runs clear.

Cut the ginger with the grain into extremely fine slivers. Soak in cold water for 2–3 minutes. Drain.

TO MAKE

Layer the sardines in a neat circle, tails to the center, in a saucepan.

Add the water and rice vinegar, cover with a drop-lid (page 143), and place over high heat.

When the liquid boils, reduce the heat to medium and simmer for 15 minutes. Press down on the drop-lid and pour off the liquid.

Add the saké, *mirin*, sugar, and half of the slivered ginger. Replace the drop-lid and

bring to a boil over high heat. Reduce heat to medium and simmer until the liquid is reduced by half (about 30 minutes).

Add the dark soy sauce and continue to simmer liquid until amount is once more halved (about 10 minutes).

Remove the drop-lid. While the sardines continue to simmer, spoon the sauce over them until it is reduced to a few tablespoons. Remove from heat.

Chop the remaining ginger. Arrange the sardines in serving bowls, top with the chopped ginger, and serve.

368 Cals

Simmered Mackerel in Miso

Saba miso-ni

The blue-backed mackerel, with its high oil content, has a strong characteristic smell, although the quantities of saké and miso here make it quite palatable. Cooked through in saké before adding the miso at the very last—

overheating is the ruin of savory miso—the mackerel should then be served immediately. Any leftovers can be oven-broiled as a casserole, the miso forming a lightly browned crust over the rich, full-bodied sauce.

Serves 4

3-inch (8-cm) piece fresh ginger (1½ oz/ 45 g)
1¾ lbs (800 g) mackerel, horse mackerel, or yellowtail fillets with skin
¾ cup (180 ml) saké
¾ cup (180 ml) water
3½ Tbsps sugar
1 tsp dark soy sauce
½ cup (120 g) red miso paste
4–6 scallions

Cut the ginger (with the grain) into very fine slivers. Soak in water for 2–3 minutes. Drain.

Use a tweezers to remove the fine bones from the fillets. Cut the fillets crosswise into 2-inch (5-cm) wide strips. Score the skin of each piece in several places. Place the fish in a bowl and pour boiling water over it. When the surface of the flesh changes color, remove to cold water, then pat dry.

Arrange the fish in a saucepan, add the saké, water, and well-drained ginger, and

Thin miso, then add to fish

cover with a drop-lid (page 143). Bring to a boil over high heat, reduce the heat to medium, and simmer for 5 minutes. Add the sugar and simmer for an additional 5 minutes. Add the soy sauce and simmer for a final 5 minutes.

Place the miso in a bowl. Use a few tablespoons of the pot liquid to thin the miso, then add miso to the fish.

Cut the scallions into 1-inch (3-cm) lengths. Add to the fish, simmer for 30 seconds, and remove from heat.

Arrange the fish and scallions in serving bowls, spoon on some sauce, and serve.

560 Cals

Stuffed Salmon
Sake kenchin-yaki

A feast for the eyes as well as the palate, pink salmon meat is complemented by eggs and by vegetables of different colors. In this version, individual servings are taken from the oven to the table in their foil wrappers—the wonderful smell at the unveiling is a treat in itself—but cut into bite-sized pieces and decoratively arranged, this makes a splendid party dish. Trout, Spanish mackerel, yellowtail, sea bass, or snapper may be substituted for salmon, and tofu for the eggs.

Serves 4

1 1-lb (450-g) salmon fillet, with skin if possible
1 Tbsp vegetable oil
4 slices lemon, rind removed

STUFFING

4 dried cloud ear mushrooms
⅓ medium carrot
2 oz (60 g) snow peas (about 20)
2 eggs
1 Tbsp *mirin*
1 tsp light soy sauce
⅓ tsp salt

TO PREPARE

Sprinkle the salmon with salt and let stand about 1 hour.

Soak the cloud ears for 1 hour (page 142).

TO MAKE

Make the STUFFING. Dice the carrot and mushrooms very finely. String the snow peas, then cut crosswise into thin slivers. Boil each vegetable separately in salted water until just tender. Refresh in cold water, then drain.

Beat the eggs lightly, combine with the *mirin*, soy sauce, and salt in a saucepan. Add the carrot and mushroom and place over medium heat. Stir occasionally. When the egg begins to set, add the snow peas. When the stuffing is half cooked, turn it out to cool.

Preheat the oven to 360° F (180° C).

Wash the salt from the salmon, remove any small bones with a tweezers, and wipe fillet dry. Place skin side down on a cutting board. Mark the fillet crosswise into 4 equal pieces. Before cutting off the first piece, make a parallel cut almost down to the skin midway between the edge and the first mark. Cut the first piece off at the mark. Spread open. Repeat, making 3 more pieces.

Prepare 4 pieces of aluminum foil 12 inches (30 cm) square. Brush the center of each piece with a thin coating of vegetable oil. Make a mound of stuffing in the center of each piece of foil. Wrap the salmon pieces, skin side up, around the stuffing. Lay 1 slice of

Cut salmon into 4 pieces

Wrap salmon around stuffing

lemon on top of the fish and wrap the aluminum foil around the stuffed fish to make neat packages.

Bake the fish in the oven for about 12 minutes.

Arrange the foil packages on serving dishes and let each diner open the foil when ready to eat. **278 Cals**

Deep-Fried Trout in Vegetable Sauce

Masu kara-age yasai-ankake

Finely scoring the trout causes it to unfold, when deep-fried, like a flower. The abundance of vegetables, the crisp texture of the trout, and the sheer smoothness of the sauce combine to give this dish a many-faceted appeal hard to match. The vegetables can be varied as desired—but avoid ones that are too watery or too pungent. Tofu or eggs can be added to the sauce to give the dish more volume, or deep-fried pork, chicken, or tofu might be easily substituted for the trout.

Serves 4

2 dried cloud ear mushrooms
vegetable oil for deep-frying
2 oz (60 g) bamboo shoots
½ medium carrot
2 oz (60 g) snow peas (about 20)
2 fresh shiitake mushrooms, washed and stems removed, or 2 fresh brown mushrooms, washed and trimmed

4 trout fillets, with skin if possible, 5 oz (150 g) each
flour
2 Tbsps finely grated fresh ginger

SAUCE

1¼ cups (300 ml) bonito stock (*dashi*) (page 140)
3½ Tbsps saké
2 Tbsps light soy sauce
2 Tbsps *mirin*
3 Tbsps cornstarch dissolved in 3 Tbsps water
2 Tbsps fresh ginger juice (page 145)

Soak the cloud ear mushrooms for 1 hour (page 142).

Preheat the oil to a high deep-frying temperature (350° F/175° C).

Cut the bamboo shoots, carrot, cloud ear mushrooms, and snow peas into 2-inch (5-cm) long julienne strips. Slice the shiitake mushrooms thinly. Boil each vegetable separately in lightly salted water until just tender (but boil the cloud ear in unsalted water). Refresh in cold water, then drain.

Score the flesh side of the trout fillets deeply, cutting near to, but not through to, the skin at ⅛-inch (¼-cm) intervals. Cut fillets into 2½-inch (6-cm) wide strips.

Dredge the fish in flour. Deep-fry until golden brown.

Combine all the SAUCE ingredients, except the ginger juice and cornstarch, in a saucepan. Add all the vegetables, then bring to a boil over high heat. Add the cornstarch dissolved in water and return to a boil. Stir in the ginger juice and immediately remove from heat.

Arrange the fish in serving bowls and add ample sauce. Top with grated ginger.

413 Cals

Score trout at close intervals, then cut

Combine vegetables and sauce, bring to a boil, and pour in cornstarch dissolved in water

39

Seafood

Stuffed Spiny Lobster

Ise-ebi denpo-yaki

A mélange of lobster meat, sliced vegetables, and beaten egg is stuffed into the lobster shells and grilled in this Japanese-style "thermidor." Though not by any means difficult, brisk cooking and attention to preparatory details will be rewarded with a delightful contrast of textures—ideally, the outside should be browned at a high temperature while the lobster meat inside remains barely heated. In place of egg, softened miso can also be used in the filling.

Serves 4

1 dried cloud ear mushroom
2 live spiny lobsters, 1 lb (450 g) each
4 fresh shiitake mushrooms, washed and stems removed, or 4 fresh brown mushrooms, washed and trimmed
¼ medium carrot
2 stalks green asparagus, trimmed
7 Tbsps bonito stock (*dashi*) (page 140)
1 Tbsp light soy sauce
1 Tbsp *mirin*
3 eggs, lightly beaten

Soak the cloud ear for 1 hour (page 142).

Cut the lobster in half lengthwise and remove the meat, reserving the shells. Cut the meat into 8 equal portions and drop in boiling water. When the surface of the meat whitens, immediately drain and plunge into ice water. Drain again and wipe dry.

Wash the shells thoroughly and boil in lightly salted water until they turn red.

Cut the shiitake (or brown) mushrooms into thin strips. Cut the cloud ear, carrot, and asparagus into 1½-inch (4-cm) long slivers.

Preheat the oven to 400° F (200° C).

Combine the bonito stock and all the vegetables in a soup pot and bring to a boil over high heat. Season with soy sauce and *mirin* and boil for about 3 minutes until the vegetables are just tender. Pour in the beaten egg in a circular motion to cover, and stir

Add beaten egg to simmering vegetables, then stir gently

Lay stuffing over lobster meat

40

gently. Cover with a drop-lid (page 143) and turn off the heat. Let stand for 2–3 minutes and then drain.

Return the lobster to the shells. Top with the egg mixture and place in the preheated oven. When the surface of the egg mixture is lightly browned, remove the lobster from oven, transfer to plates, and serve.

310 Cals

Saké-Simmered Lobster

Omaru-ebi gusoku-ni

The Japanese name for this recipe literally translates as "lobster in armor," but properly prepared it won't put up a fight. The bare minimum of simmering over high heat ensures that the meat will stay deliciously tender; the lobster is done when the meat can be easily separated from the shell.

Serves 4

2 live lobsters, about 1 lb (450 g) each
2 leeks
4 oz (120 g) watercress
3–4 inches (8–10 cm) fresh ginger (1½ oz/ 45 g)
1 Tbsp fresh ginger juice (page 145)
chervil leaves

FOR SIMMERING

1⅔ cups (400 ml) saké
¾ cup (180 ml) water
7 Tbsps *mirin*
2 Tbsps dark soy sauce
2 Tbsps light soy sauce
2 Tbsps sugar
½ tsp salt

TO PREPARE

Cut the live lobsters in half lengthwise and then cut each half into 2–3 pieces.

Cut the leeks into ½-inch (1½-cm) rounds, boil in salted water until just tender, and drain.

Blanch the watercress in lightly salted boiling water, drain, and refresh in cold water. Drain again and cut into 1½-inch (4-cm) lengths.

Slice the ginger with the grain into very fine slivers and soak in cold water for 2–3 minutes.

Place the saké and water in a pan and bring to a boil over high heat, then add all the remaining SIMMERING ingredients. Add the lobster and cover with a drop-lid (page 143). Boil for 5–6 minutes over high heat until the meat can be easily removed from the shell. Ladle simmering liquid over lobster several times. Add the leek and watercress. Heat through, add the ginger juice, and immediately remove from heat.

Divide the lobster and vegetables among 4 bowls. Pour in an ample amount of sauce. Top with well-drained ginger, garnish with chervil, and serve.

395 Cals

Whole Prawns Grilled in the Shell

Ebi onigara-yaki

Fresh, medium-large prawns (1 oz/30 g) grilled over a high flame can be eaten shell and all—what's more the crunchy shells have a subtle sweetness that lends a nutty flavor to the inner meat. Larger prawns may, of course, require separating the meat from the shell after cooking to facilitate eating. Prawns grilled in the shell with plain salt and topped with lemon juice can be every bit as delicious as cooking with the sauce given here.

Skewer prawns

Pour sauce over prawns just before they are done

Serves 4

8 prawns, 1 oz (30 g) each

TURNIP GARNISH

1 medium turnip
2-inch (5-cm) length kelp (*konbu*)
½ cup (120 ml) rice vinegar
½ cup (120 ml) water
4 tsps sugar
pinch salt
2 dried red chili peppers
zest from 1 lemon, slivered

TERIYAKI SAUCE

1 cup (240 ml) *mirin*
⅔ cup (160 ml) saké
½ cup (120 ml) dark soy sauce
3 Tbsps tamari soy sauce (or increase soy sauce and *mirin* by 3 Tbsps each)

12 long metal skewers (if grilling)

TO PREPARE

Begin preparing the TURNIP GARNISH 1½–2 hours before serving, following the instructions for Turnip Chrysanthemums (page 141), but cutting the turnip into ¾-inch (2-cm) cubes, scoring finely in one direction, and adding the lemon zest when soaking turnip in marinade.

Combine all TERIYAKI SAUCE ingredients, bring to a boil over high heat, reduce heat to low, and simmer until the volume is slightly reduced (about 10 percent). Skim occasionally.

TO MAKE

Carefully cut through the shell along the back of each prawn and spread open. Pick out the dark vein.

Grill or bake prawns.

Grilling: Thread a pair of prawns on a set of 3 skewers so that the sharp ends flare out and the blunt ends meet and may be easily gripped in one hand. Grill over a hot gas flame for about 3 minutes. When they are almost done, remove the prawns from the flame and pour on ample Teriyaki Sauce, placing a bowl underneath to catch the excess sauce. Continue cooking until the sauce dries, pour on sauce a second time, and finish cooking.

Baking: Preheat the oven to 400° F (200° C). Place the prawns on a wire rack and cook for 5 minutes. Pour on the Teriyaki Sauce and cook until the sauce dries. Pour sauce over again, cook for a few more seconds, then remove from heat.

Remove the skewers. Arrange the shrimp shell side down in dishes. Finish the Turnip Garnish by draining and topping with lemon zest. Place alongside the shrimp.

194 Cals

Squid Teriyaki

Ika teriyaki

Excessive cooking can turn squid tough and rubbery, so the key here is to work quickly, grilling over a high flame so that the cooking stops just as the heat reaches the center meat. Also, scoring the surface of the squid gives the sauce more chance to penetrate and makes the squid easier to eat. When following the fry-pan method, be sure to dust the squid lightly with flour to keep the sauce from spattering. For another teriyaki dish, see Yellowtail Teriyaki (page 35).

Serves 4

1 lb (450 g) squid, cleaned and skinned (page 141)
12 small sweet green peppers or 2 bell peppers
flour (if pan-frying)
1–2 Tbsps vegetable oil

TERIYAKI SAUCE

1 cup (240 ml) *mirin*
⅔ cup (160 ml) saké
½ cup (120 ml) dark soy sauce

3 Tbsps tamari soy sauce (or increase dark soy sauce and *mirin* by 3 Tbsps each)

long metal skewers (if grilling)

Combine all the TERIYAKI SAUCE ingredients in a saucepan and bring to a boil over high heat. Reduce heat to low and simmer, skimming occasionally, until the volume is reduced slightly (about 10 percent).

Score the outside of the squid in a shallow diamond pattern.

Turn the squid over and insert 3 to 5 skewers (depending on the size of the squid), allowing them to protrude occasionally from the flesh, as if you were sewing the squid. Insert a last skewer at a slight angle across the other skewers to prevent the squid from curling while cooking. (If pan-frying the squid, skip this step.)

Remove the stems from the small green peppers (or seed the bell peppers and cut each one into 6 strips). Skewer 3-4 pieces together on 2 or 3 skewers. (If pan-frying peppers, do not skewer.)

Grill or pan-fry the squid.

Grilling: Grill each side of the squid over a very hot gas flame for 2 minutes. Just before it is done remove the squid from the flame and pour a generous amount of sauce over the squid (put a bowl below to catch excess sauce), and dry over flame. Repeat 2-3 times.

Pan-frying: Cut the cleaned squid into ½-inch (1½-cm) rounds. Dust with flour. Heat 1 Tbsp of vegetable oil in a frying pan over high heat and fry the squid. Brown both sides slightly, then remove the squid to a colander and douse with hot water to remove oil. In a clean saucepan, simmer ½ cup (120 ml) Teriyaki Sauce over low heat until it thickens slightly and becomes sticky. Add the squid to the pan and coat with the sauce. Heat for a few seconds and remove the squid from the pan.

Wipe the peppers with vegetable oil, sprinkle with salt, and grill over a hot flame until they become tender—only a minute or so—or pan-fry in vegetable oil.

Remove the skewers from both squid and peppers. Cut the squid into ¾ × 1½-inch (2 × 4-cm) rectangles.

Arrange the squid and pepper in serving dishes.

270 Cals

Score squid in a diamond pattern

Add a last skewer crosswise to prevent curling

Douse with sauce when almost done

Clams Grilled in the Shell

Yaki hamaguri

This is an extremely simple way of cooking that makes use of the natural salt in the clams themselves, but care must be taken to avoid overcooking. Small clams may be grilled right in the shell; large clams must first be cut into pieces. In either case, cooking should stop just as foam starts to issue from the shells. Oysters, mussels, scallops, and most other bivalves can also be grilled in this manner.

Serves 4

8 live hard-shell clams, about 2 oz (60 g) each

salt

juice from 1 lemon

TO PREPARE

When buying the clams, inspect them carefully. Avoid those with broken or cracked shells, or any that do not shut tightly when touched.

Let the clams stand in salted water (1 tsp salt to 3 cups [700 ml] water) in a cool, dark place for 5–6 hours to allow them to expel sand.

TO MAKE

Cut away the black hinge ligaments visible at the back of the shell. Working over a bowl to catch the juice, insert a knife between the lips of the shell and release the ligament by twisting shells. Carefully scrape the meat from the shells. Reserve the shells and strain the clam juice to clarify (page 142).

Trim away clinging material from clam meat. Cut the body meat in half horizontally and remove and discard blackish organs. Remove the tough outer membrane from the trimmed portion and discard, then cut the thin flesh into ½-inch (1½-cm) lengths.

Make several incisions along the edge of the thinner side of the body meat.

Separate the shell halves and wash well. Divide the pieces of clam among 8 shell halves. Pour in some of the clam juice and cover with the remaining shell halves. Sprinkle some salt on the outside of the shells (for decoration) and grill on a wire net (or barbecue) over high heat.

When the clam juice boils and foam shows at the lips of the shells, remove from heat immediately. Arrange 2 shells in each dish, add lemon juice to taste, and serve.

75 Cals

Cut off black ligaments

Slide knife between lips of shell and twist shell back and forth to open

Trim clam meat of clinging matter, membrane, and organs

Cut at regular intervals along meat fringe

Vinegared Crab

Kanisu

In Japan, the opening of crab season signals the coming of winter. A typical way of preparing crab is in a vinaigrette sauce as here. For the best flavor, serve the crabmeat in large chunks as soon as it becomes cool enough to shell. The red crabmeat, green cucumber slices, and dark green wakame look exquisite together, and the tangy Ginger-Vinegar Dressing is sure to stimulate any appetite. If no fresh ginger is available, a dressing of lemon or lime juice and soy sauce makes a fine substitute.

Serves 4

⅓ oz (10 g) dried *wakame* seaweed

1 1-lb (450-g) fresh crab (or ½ lb [220 g] frozen crabmeat and a dash of saké)

1 cucumber

2-inch (5-cm) length kelp (*konbu*)

GINGER-VINEGAR DRESSING

½ cup (120 ml) bonito stock (*dashi*) (page 140)

7 Tbsps rice vinegar

5 tsps light soy sauce

4 tsps sugar

5 tsps fresh ginger juice (page 145)

Soften and prepare the *wakame* seaweed (page 143). Chop into 1-inch (2-cm) lengths.

Pull away the apron on the underside of the crab with your fingers. Place the crab in a pot with ample salted water, cover with a drop-lid (page 143), bring to a boil over high heat, reduce heat to medium, and simmer for 18–20 minutes. (If using frozen crab, sprinkle with a little saké, steam over high heat for 10 minutes, and pick out any shell and cartilage.)

Drain and let cool, shell side down.

Peel the cucumber, quarter it lengthwise, and scrape out the seeds. Slice thinly crosswise. Add the *konbu* kelp to salted water (1½ tsps salt to 1 cup [240 ml] water) and soak the cucumber.

Combine all the GINGER-VINEGAR DRESSING ingredients, except the ginger juice, in a saucepan. Bring to a boil over high heat, then force-cool rapidly by placing the pan in a bowl of ice water. Add the ginger juice and mix well.

When the crab is cool, pull off the hood and cut off the legs. Discard intestines and other inedible parts. Pick out the yellow eggs (if any) to be served later if desired. Chop off legs. Cut the body in half crosswise, then cut each piece in half horizontally. Pick out the crabmeat. Cut the legs and claws lengthwise and pick out the meat.

To serve, drain the cucumber, discarding the *konbu* kelp, and squeeze out any excess water from the cucumber with your fingers. Arrange the crab (and eggs, if desired), cucumber, and *wakame* seaweed in serving bowls, spoon on a few tablespoon of the dressing, and serve.

110 Cals

46

Pull off apron before cooking

Pull off hood of boiled crab

Remove inedible parts

Take out eggs

Cut off legs

Quarter crab

Remove meat from shell

Shrimp and Leeks with Mustard-Miso Sauce

Ebi to riku no karashi-su-miso-kake

Miso is used in a number of toppings for Japanese "salads," but Mustard-Miso Sauce is definitely the most popular. A harmonious blend of mellow miso and tart rice vinegar, with a dash of mustard for tang, the amber-colored sauce makes a lovely complement to the shrimp and leeks. Consider this as an actual salad and endless possibilities present themselves: squid, oysters, mussels, scallops, and other shellfish, or even chicken may be substituted for the shrimp; in place of the leeks, try scallions, zucchini, asparagus, broccoli, or other green vegetables. One sauce covers all.

Serves 4

8 raw shrimp, 1 oz (30 g) each
1 leek
tarragon

MUSTARD-MISO SAUCE

1 egg yolk
5 Tbsps nonsweet white miso paste
3 Tbsps sugar
2½ Tbsps rice vinegar

2 Tbsps bonito stock (*dashi*) (page 140)
1½ tsps hot yellow mustard (*karashi*) or any mustard that is not sweet or vinegary
1 tsp light soy sauce

8 bamboo skewers

Devein the shrimp, then skewer on the underside from head to tail. Drop in lightly salted boiling water for 3 minutes. Transfer to cold water, cool, remove the skewers, and pat the shrimp dry.

Shell the shrimp and remove the head and tail. Cut into 1-inch (3-cm) pieces.

Cut the leek into ½-inch (1½-cm) rounds. Boil until just tender, drain, sprinkle with salt, and let cool.

Combine all the MUSTARD-MISO SAUCE ingredients in a double boiler and heat, stirring constantly, until the sauce thickens to a mayonnaise-like consistency.

Make a bed of sauce on the serving dish. Set the leek and shrimp on the sauce and garnish with tarragon.

138 Cals

Devein shrimp by inserting toothpick between shell segments

Skewer shrimp on underside from head to tail with bamboo skewer

Scallops and Kiwi Fruit with Three-Flavors Dressing

Hotate-gai to kiui no sanbai-zu

The kiwi fruit has enjoyed immense popularity in Japan in recent years, giving birth to new tastes in Japanese cooking. Succulent yet subtly tart, the kiwi fruit makes a remarkable contribution to vinegared dishes such as this. Care must be taken, however, not to crush the fruit, or the bitterness in the seeds will be released; here, the texture of the fruit is preserved in petit cubes. Other fruits that work well in vinegared dishes include mangoes, strawberries, and grated apple.

Serves 4

½ cucumber

4 shucked scallops of sashimi quality, 2 oz (60 g) each

¼ tomato

2 kiwi fruit

THREE-FLAVORS DRESSING

7 Tbsps rice vinegar

7 Tbsps bonito stock (*dashi*) (page 140)

1 Tbsp light soy sauce

1 Tbsp sugar

½ tsp salt

Peel the cucumber, slice in half lengthwise, and scrape out the seeds. Slice thinly crosswise. Soak the slices in salted water (1½ tsps salt to 1 cup [240 ml] water) for about 20 minutes. When they have become tender, drain and squeeze out excess water with your hands.

Combine all the ingredients for THREE-FLAVORS DRESSING in a saucepan. Bring to a boil over high heat and immediately set the pan in a bowl of ice water and cool.

Remove the tough ligament and surrounding membrane from the scallops if it has not already been done. Slice each scallop into 3 rounds.

Peel, seed, and chop the tomato coarsely.

Peel the kiwi fruit and cut into ¼-inch (½-cm) cubes. Combine with dressing.

Pour some of the dressing with kiwi fruit into serving dishes and arrange a portion of scallop on top. Garnish with well-drained cucumber and tomato.

86 Cals

49

Beef and Pork

Grilled Beef

Gyuniku ami-yaki

A technique prominent in Japanese cuisine is that of ami-yaki—literally "net grilling"—in which meat, fish, or vegetables are grilled on a wire net over a high flame or red-hot coals. In the case of meat, the key point is to sear only the outside surface, leaving a touch of red inside. Here high-quality, well-marbled cuts have been used, but for a lighter taste, use fillet or leaner cuts of sirloin, or try using this method for chicken, pork (grill well, of course), or duck. Though the beef is served with two complementary dressings—a rich sesame sauce and the light, refreshing Lemon-Soy Dipping Sauce—it is also wonderful with a good mustard or lemon juice and salt.

Serves 4

1 lb (450 g) well-marbled sirloin or tenderloin beef

8 fresh shiitake mushrooms, washed and stems removed, or 8 fresh brown mushrooms, washed and trimmed

2 white long onions or ½ medium onion

8 small sweet green peppers or 2 bell peppers

LEMON-SOY DIPPING SAUCE (*Ponzu*)

7 Tbsps lemon juice

7 Tbsps dark soy sauce

5 Tbsps rice vinegar

5 tsps *mirin*, alcohol burned off (page 146)

1 Tbsp tamari soy sauce (see Note)

¼ cup loose bonito flakes (⅙ oz/5 g)

1-inch (2½-cm) length kelp (*konbu*)

SESAME DIPPING SAUCE

2 Tbsps white sesame paste (page 140)

1 Tbsp sugar

4 Tbsps dark soy sauce

1 Tbsp *mirin*, alcohol burned off (page 146)

2 Tbsps saké, alcohol burned off (page 147)

3 Tbsps bonito stock (*dashi*) (page 140)

TO PREPARE

Make the LEMON-SOY DIPPING SAUCE: Mix together all the ingredients and refrigerate for 24 hours to allow flavor to fully mature. Strain to clarify (page 142).

Combine all the SESAME DIPPING SAUCE ingredients in a blender and whir to a smooth paste (or grind sesame paste in a mortar and pestle, then add the remaining ingredients in order and one by one, grinding as you go).

TO MAKE

Slice the beef into ¼ × ¾ × 2-inch (½ × 2 × 5-cm) strips. Score the mushroom caps with a shallow diamond pattern. Score the long onions and then cut into 1-inch (3-cm) lengths (or cut the onion into ½-inch [1-cm] slices and secure the rings with a toothpick or bamboo skewer). Remove the stems from the small sweet green peppers (or core, seed, and cut the bell peppers into 8 strips).

Grill the vegetables and meat over hot coals (or on a wire net over a hot gas flame). Grill the meat as desired; grill the vegetables until the surface of each is just tender (the onion should be slightly translucent).

Serve a bowl of each sauce to each diner. Eat the food hot from the grill.

431 Cals

NOTE: If you do not have tamari soy sauce, make a simple, flavored soy sauce instead of the Lemon-Soy Dipping Sauce. Combine 7 Tbsps dark soy sauce, ⅓ cup (80 ml) saké with alcohol burned off (page 147), 7 Tbsps lemon juice, 1-inch (2½-cm) length kelp, and ¼ cup loose bonito flakes (⅙ oz/5 g). Refrigerate for 24 hours. Strain to clarify (page 142).

Beef Tartare, Japanese Style

Gyuniku tataki-zukuri

Originally, the tataki method was used exclusively for preparing Quick-Seared Bonito Sashimi (page 26), which with all its variations is famous in its own right. Thick fillets of bonito are passed over a high flame or red-hot coals, and the resultant border of scorched flesh contrasts vividly with the bright red core, offering subtle, but distinct, counterpoints in color and taste.

Here the same method is used for beef. Skewering the slices of high-grade beef and passing them over direct heat is the ideal method, but a similar effect can be obtained by searing them in a frying pan that has been lightly brushed with oil. In this method too, the highest possible heat and utmost speed are essential. The beef is served with a piquant Lemon-Soy Dipping Sauce. Different effects can be achieved by making the slices somewhat thicker and serving them with either wasabi horseradish or hot yellow mustard (karashi) in soy sauce.

Serves 4

1 lb (450 g) very fresh lean sirloin, tenderloin, or fillet of beef
1 Tbsp dark soy sauce
1 Tbsp saké

LEMON-SOY DIPPING SAUCE (*Ponzu*)

7 Tbsps lemon juice
7 Tbsps dark soy sauce
5 Tbsps rice vinegar
1 Tbsp tamari soy sauce (see Note, page 51)
5 tsps *mirin*, alcohol burned off (page 146)
¼ cup loose bonito flakes (⅙ oz/5 g)
1-inch (2½-cm) length kelp (*konbu*)

CONDIMENTS

4 Tbsps finely chopped and rinsed scallion
4 Tbsps Red Maple Radish (page 140)
3 tsps grated fresh ginger root

GARNISHES

4 "buds" *myoga* ginger or 2 lettuce leaves
4 *shiso* or mint leaves, trimmed

long metal skewers

TO PREPARE

Combine all the LEMON-SOY DIPPING SAUCE ingredients, mix well, and refrigerate for 24 hours to allow flavor to fully mature. Strain to clarify (page 142).

TO MAKE

Sliver the *myoga* ginger and soak in cold water (or shred the lettuce and set aside).

Cut the beef into ½-inch (1½-cm) thick slices and trim excess fat. Thread each slice on 2 or 3 skewers, fanning them out into the meat.

Sprinkle both sides with salt. Grill each side over a hot gas flame very briefly (about 30 seconds) until the outside is slightly singed. Immediately remove from heat and plunge into ice water.

When the meat has cooled, remove the skewers and pat dry. Mix together the soy sauce and saké and sprinkle over the meat. Wrap in plastic wrap and refrigerate for 1 hour.

TO SERVE

Cut the meat into very thin (about ⅛-inch/ ¼-cm) slices. Arrange the meat on a serving dish, garnish with *shiso* (or mint) leaves, and make mounds of the chopped scallion, *myoga* ginger (or lettuce), Red Maple Radish, and grated ginger root. Serve a bowl of Lemon-Soy Dip to each diner. Season the dip with condiments to taste.

395 Cals

After meat is skewered, sprinkle with salt

Grill both sides over gas flame

Cool grilled meat in ice water

53

Grilled Beef with Miso

Gyuniku miso-yaki

The cuisine of miso-yaki, in which fish is coated with miso and grilled over a direct flame or charcoal, has been passed down for generations. Here this method has been adopted for beef with excellent results. The miso eliminates unpleasant tastes and brings out the mellow flavor and aroma of the marbling. Grill the meat, coat it with miso sauce, and for a final flavorful touch slip it into the broiler until the miso begins to darken and brown.

Serves 4

1 lb (450 g) tenderloin or fillet of beef
1 medium zucchini, about ½ lb (220 g)
4 Tbsps Red Miso Sauce (page 85)
2–3 tsps poppy seeds, toasted in same way
 as sesame seeds (page 140)
2 Tbsps vegetable oil
4 sprigs watercress

long metal skewers

Cut the beef into ½ × 1 × 2-inch (1 × 2½ × 5-cm) pieces.

Peel the zucchini, slice in half lengthwise, then cut into ½-inch (1-cm) half moons.

Skewer 2 pieces of beef on a pair of skewers, sprinkle lightly with salt, and grill over high heat until the surface of the meat has browned, then turn and grill the other side. Remove the skewers and spread a generous amount of Red Miso Sauce on each piece.

Line a shallow baking pan or ovenproof casserole with aluminum foil and arrange the beef in the bottom. Place under a very hot broiler until the miso begins to brown slightly. Remove and top with poppy seeds.

Heat the oil in a frying pan over medium heat and sauté the zucchini. When tender, season with salt and pepper, and remove from heat.

Arrange the beef and zucchini in serving dishes, garnish with a sprig of watercress, and serve.

283 Cals

Spread miso topping over grilled beef

Simmered Beef with Vegetables

Gyuniku to yasai no uma-ni

This is a variation on one of the simple one-pot recipes that are part of every Japanese home-cooking repertoire. The traditional method calls for chicken, but with beef a richer, fuller flavor has been achieved. Meat and vegetables are simmered together in a single saucepan. The flavors of the simmering liquid are on the light side, so serve generous amounts with the meat and vegetables. If it is simmered over a low flame until the liquid is darker and heavier, this dish may be kept in the refrigerator for two or three days.

Serves 4

4 dried shiitake mushrooms
3½-inch (9-cm) piece fresh ginger (1½ oz/ 45 g)
½ lb (220 g) tenderloin or fillet of beef
4 oz (120 g) canned bamboo shoots
¼ medium carrot
½ acorn squash
2 oz (60 g) green beans
1 Tbsp vegetable oil

FOR SIMMERING

2 cups (480 ml) bonito stock (*dashi*) (page 140) or chicken stock (page 22)
7 Tbsps saké
2 Tbsps sugar
1 Tbsp *mirin*
4 tsps dark soy sauce
2 tsps light soy sauce

Soak the mushrooms for 6–7 hours (page 142). Quarter the caps.

Cut the ginger with the grain into very fine slivers. Soak in cold water for 2–3 minutes, then drain.

Cut the beef into bite-sized cubes.

Prepare the remaining vegetables: Wash the bamboo shoots well, removing any white residue. Trim the carrot. Peel and seed the acorn squash. Trim the green beans if necessary. Cut all the vegetables, except the green beans, into bite-sized pieces and parboil each vegetable separately in lightly salted water until just tender. Refresh in cold water and drain. Cut the green beans into 1-inch (2½-cm) lengths.

Heat the oil in a saucepan over high heat. Add the beef, then sauté, stirring constantly, until it begins to brown.

Add the carrot, bamboo shoot, mushroom, acorn squash, bonito (or chicken) stock, saké, and *half* the ginger (reserve green beans). Cover with a drop-lid (page 143). Bring to a boil, reduce heat to low, and simmer 7–8 minutes. Add the sugar and *mirin* and simmer for 5 more minutes. Add the dark and light soy sauce and simmer for a final 5 minutes. Remove from heat, stir in the green beans, sprinkle on remaining ginger, and serve.

276 Cals

Rolled Beef and Asparagus

Gyuniku asupara-maki koro-ni

One of the traditional dishes of Japan is Yawata-maki, in which rolls made by wrapping burdock root with fillets of eel are grilled with sweet sauce. This adaptation uses asparagus and beef instead of the traditional ingredients, which are often hard to find. Far from a mere compromise, however, the contrast of flavors offered by the rich marinated beef and the light taste of the asparagus make this a tantalizing variation on its traditional ancestor. The flavors remain relatively unchanged after cooling, so this is an excellent party dish. Thin slices of chicken, pork, or duck may be substituted for beef, and celery, green beans, or scallions are good alternatives to asparagus.

Serves 4

1-lb (450-g) block beef sirloin, thinly sliced
8 stalks green asparagus, trimmed
2 Tbsps vegetable oil
hot yellow mustard (*karashi*) or any mustard that is not sweet or vinegary

SAUCE
⅔ cup (160 ml) saké
3 Tbsps dark soy sauce
2½ Tbsps sugar
2 Tbsps *mirin*
1 Tbsp tamari soy sauce (optional)

Combine all of the SAUCE ingredients. Marinate the beef in the sauce for 15 minutes.

Quarter the asparagus lengthwise and parboil in lightly salted water. Refresh in cold water, drain, and pat dry.

Remove the beef, reserve the sauce, and lay out 2 or 3 pieces of beef so that they overlap lengthwise. Lay 4 to 5 pieces of asparagus across the meat and roll up. Tie each roll in several places with kitchen string.

Heat the oil in a pan over medium heat and sauté the beef rolls. When the beef is lightly and evenly browned, add the reserved sauce. Simmer for 1 minute and remove the rolls. Reduce heat slightly and continue simmering the sauce, stirring occasionally, until the liquid is reduced and the sauce begins to thicken. Return the beef rolls to the pan and shake to coat evenly. Remove the rolls.

Carefully cut away the string. Slice the rolls into 1-inch (2½-cm) rounds and arrange in dishes. Add some mustard to each dish and serve hot or at room temperature.

518 Cals

Roll asparagus in beef and tie roll with string

Beef Salad

Gyuniku sarada

Combining parboiled slices of beef and a rich variety of vegetables, this is an ideal summer salad, or if served in petit portions it makes a distinctive hors d'oeuvre. With the addition of sesame and ginger to what is fundamentally Three-Flavors Dressing (page 49), this vinaigrette sauce takes on new dimensions. The piquant aromas of toasted sesame and freshly grated ginger are fully exploited, the last also adding a zesty accent. Well-cooked pork or chicken may be substituted for beef, and the meat may be cooked to taste.

Serves 4

⅓ oz (10 g) dried *wakame* seaweed

1 lb (450 g) very fresh tenderloin or fillet of beef

½ cucumber

2 stalks celery

⅓ medium carrot

8 red radishes

DRESSING

½ cup (120 ml) bonito stock (*dashi*) (page 140)

7 Tbsps rice vinegar

4 Tbsps dark soy sauce

2 Tbsps sugar

4 Tbsps white sesame seeds, toasted (page 140)

1 Tbsp finely grated fresh ginger

Soak and prepare the *wakame* seaweed (page 143). Cut into 1-inch (3-cm) lengths.

Begin making the DRESSING: Combine the bonito stock, vinegar, soy sauce, and sugar in a saucepan, bring to a boil over high heat, remove from heat, and cool rapidly by placing the pan in a bowl of ice water. Set aside.

Cut the beef into bars with 1-inch (3-cm) square cross-sections. Drop in boiling water. When the color changes (about 30 seconds), drain and drop in ice water. Cool, drain, pat dry, and slice crosswise.

Peel the cucumber, quarter lengthwise, and seed. String the celery. Cut the vegetables into fine julienne strips. Soak each vegetable separately in water.

Finish the DRESSING: Whir the sesame seeds in a blender (or grind them in a mortar and pestle) until they begin to lose their shape—a rough paste with some pieces of whole sesame remaining. Add the bonito stock mixture and grated ginger and mix.

To serve, drain the vegetables, then arrange the beef, vegetables, and *wakame* seaweed in dishes and set out the dressing.

224 Cals

Nagasaki-Style Braised Pork

Buta kaku-ni

This dish is famous as an example of Ship-poku cuisine, the unique "Chinese-style" culinary art developed in Nagasaki between the seventeenth and nineteenth centuries, when Nagasaki was Japan's only open port. A Japanese adaptation of Chinese Dongpo Pork, this recipe calls for the pork to be simmered twice: first for a lengthy period in milk or a stock of tofu pulp to remove the stronger flavors, and then in a dark, rich bonito stock until the pork is unbelievably tender.

Serves 4

2 lbs (1 kg) boneless pork belly
2 Tbsps vegetable oil
1 cup (250 g) unpacked *okara* (tofu pulp) or milk (see below) (optional)
3½ oz (100 g) fresh ginger, thinly sliced
8 raw pickling (pearl) onions
1 cup (130 g) shelled green peas
hot yellow mustard (*karashi*) or any mustard that is not sweet or vinegary

FOR SIMMERING

2½ cups (600 ml) bonito stock (*dashi*) (page 140)
¾ cup (180 ml) saké
4½ Tbsps sugar
4 Tbsps dark soy sauce
2 tsps tamari soy sauce (optional)

Cut the pork into 1½-inch (4-cm) cubes. Heat the oil in a frying pan over high heat and stir-fry the pork briefly until the surface turns brown. Transfer to a colander and pour ample boiling water over it to remove any oil.

Place the pork, *okara* plus ample water (or half milk and half water or just water) to cover, and *half* the sliced ginger in a soup pot over high heat and cover with a drop-lid (page 143). Bring to a boil, reduce heat to low, and simmer for 30–40 minutes.

Remove from heat and, leaving the drop-lid in place, gradually add cold water to cool. Let stand 15–20 minutes under a thin stream of cold running water. Remove all the *okara*.

Boil the onions until just tender in lightly salted water, drop in cold water to refresh, and drain.

Rub the green peas with salt and then boil in lightly salted water until just tender. Remove from heat and gradually add water to the pan to cool and prevent the peas from wrinkling. Drain.

Drain the pork. Combine in a soup pot with the bonito stock, saké, and remaining ginger, then cover with a drop-lid and bring to a boil over high heat. Reduce heat to low and simmer for 10 minutes. Add the sugar and simmer for 5 more minutes. Add the soy sauce and simmer for an additional 5 minutes. Add the tamari soy sauce, onions, and green peas, simmer for a final 2 minutes, remove to serving plates, and serve with mustard.

975 Cals

Deep-Fried Stuffed Pork

Buta rosu kawari-age

Ever since its introduction from the West, the pork cutlet has undergone a steady Japanization, until today in its present deep-fried form it is the undisputed king of Japanese-style "Western" cuisine. Here a transformation has been worked on it by stuffing thin slices of pork with the aromatic Gruyère cheese and celery and then deep-frying it. A little lemon and salt is more than enough to bring out the flavors of the cheese and celery. Many other stuffings suggest themselves: scallions, ginger, sautéed onion, bacon, pickles, mustard, and so on.

Serves 4

1 lb (450 g) boneless pork loin
4 fresh shiitake mushrooms, washed and
    stems removed, or 4 fresh brown mush-
    rooms, washed and trimmed
2 large outer cabbage leaves
½ stalk celery
3½ oz (100 g) Gruyère cheese
vegetable oil for deep-frying
flour

⅓ oz (10 g) cellophane noodles (*harusame*)
2 Tbsps white sesame seeds, toasted (page 140)
egg white, lightly beaten
1 Tbsp butter
4 lemon wedges

Cut the pork into 12 slices, each ½ inch (1 cm) thick.

Score the mushroom caps in a diamond pattern, then cut in half. Cut the cabbage leaves into 1-inch (3-cm) squares. String the celery. Cut the celery and cheese into ½-inch (1-cm) wide strips about the same length as the pork slices.

Preheat the oil to a medium deep-frying temperature (340° F/170° C).

Slice open the pork horizontally so that it is only ¼ inch (½ cm) thick and has twice the surface area. Be careful not to cut completely in half. Open and sprinkle the inside with flour. Stuff with the cheese and celery. Close the meat over the stuffing and press edges lightly.

Cut the noodles with a scissors into very short (¼-inch/½-cm) pieces and mix with the sesame seeds.

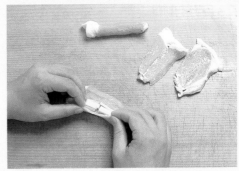

Stuff pork slices with cheese and celery bits

Coat the stuffed pork slices first in flour, then in lightly beaten egg white, and finally in the sesame-noodle mixture.

Deep-fry the stuffed pork for about 3 minutes or until golden brown. Remove from the oil, sprinkle with salt while still hot, and drain on absorbent paper.

Melt the butter in a saucepan over high heat and sauté the mushrooms. Season with salt and pepper to taste.

Cut the stuffed pork in half and arrange in serving dish. Add cabbage, sautéed mushroom, and a lemon wedge.

575 Cals

Chicken

Yakitori

Along with sushi, tempura, and sukiyaki, yakitori already enjoys worldwide popularity as a representative of Japanese cuisine, and its tender, petit morsels are fondly remembered by all who have sampled them during a trip to Japan. In Japan it is primarily a snack served with drinks—a snack whose popularity is clear from the innumerable yakitori bars throughout the country. It makes a good hors d'oeuvre at any party and is perfect for barbecues since it can be served hot off the grill. Few people can resist the rich sauce featured here, but it is also interesting to grill the chicken with just a sprinkling of salt and serve it with lemon and mustard.

Serves 4

½ lb (220 g) chicken skin
1 lb (450 g) boned chicken thigh
½ lb (220 g) chicken livers
½ lb (220 g) chicken gizzards
2 white long onions or 4–6 scallions
4 bell peppers

YAKITORI SAUCE

the bones of two chickens
3½ cups (800 ml) dark soy sauce
3½ cups (800 ml) *mirin*
1⅔ cups (400 ml) saké
7–9 oz (200–260 g) rock sugar
½ cup (120 ml) tamari soy sauce (or increase *mirin* by ¼ cup [60 ml] and dark soy sauce by 7 Tbsps)

CHICKEN BALLS

10 oz (300 g) ground chicken
1 egg, lightly beaten
1 tsp fresh ginger juice (page 145)
2 Tbsps cornstarch dissolved in 2 Tbsps water
2-inch (5-cm) length kelp (*konbu*)

CONDIMENTS

ground *sansho* pepper
salt
hot yellow mustard (*karashi*) or any mustard that is not sweet or vinegary
lemon wedges

20–30 bamboo skewers

Make the YAKITORI SAUCE: Bake the chicken bones in a 400° F (200° C) oven until golden brown (30–40 minutes). Place the baked bones in a large soup pot along with all the other sauce ingredients. Simmer over low heat until the sauce is reduced by 10 percent (about 1 hour).

While the sauce is simmering prepare the meat and vegetables. Make the CHICKEN BALLS first: Place the ground chicken in a food processor, whir to mince, add the remaining ingredients (except kelp), and whir to a smooth paste (or grind the chicken in a mortar and pestle and then mix in the egg, ginger juice, and cornstarch one at a time). Add the kelp to an ample amount of water and warm over high heat. Adjust the flame so that the water remains just below the boiling point. Roll the mixture into 1-inch (2½-cm) balls. Add to water. When the balls rise to the surface, cook 2–3 minutes longer, then drain and allow to cool.

Boil the chicken skin until it is cooked. Cut into 1-inch (2½-cm) squares.

Cut the boned thigh into 1-inch (2½-cm) squares.

Wash the chicken livers well, then cut into 1-inch (2½-cm) squares. Remove the tough white material, then cut the gizzards into 1-inch (2½-cm) squares.

Cut the white portion of the long onions (or scallions) into 1-inch (2½-cm) lengths. Core, seed, and cut the bell peppers into 1-inch (2½-cm) squares.

Make seven types of yakitori skewers: gizzards, chicken and long onion (or scallion), liver, chicken and bell pepper, chicken, chicken balls, and skin. Skewered pieces should be touching. (If using scallion, alternate 3 pieces of scallion with 1 piece chicken and press scallion pieces together tightly to prevent excessive scorching and to retard cooking time so that they will finish with the chicken.)

TO GRILL AND SERVE

Barbecue the skewered food. Grill the meat on both sides. When the meat is cooked through, dip the skewers in the sauce (or baste). Grill to dry the sauce, dip again, and serve. To make salted yakitori, sprinkle some skewers with salt and grill (do not use sauce). Be careful not to overcook the yakitori—the finished meat should be tender, not dry.

Sprinkle the yakitori with *sansho* pepper if desired and serve. Provide salt, mustard, and lemon wedges for diners to season yakitori as desired.

If you wish, complement the yakitori with a platter of mixed raw vegetables such as carrots, celery, and cabbage.

866 Cals

NOTE: Yakitori sauce can be made in large quantities and kept indefinitely unrefrigerated. After each use simmer the sauce and strain to clarify (page 142) and to remove moisture and food particles. Store in a cool, dark place in a tightly sealed container.

Soft-Simmered Chicken

Tori yawaraka-ni

Chicken legs simmered slowly with konbu kelp yield a rich stock. This is then seasoned and the chicken simmered further to allow the flavors to seep into the meat. The sprinkle of pepper just before serving provides the final accent.

Serves 4

2½ lbs (1.2 kg) chicken legs (thighs and drumsticks)
2-inch (5-cm) length kelp (*konbu*)
2 white long onions or 5 scallions
1 oz (30 g) snow peas (about 12)

FOR SIMMERING

5 cups (1.2 L) water
7 Tbsps saké
2 Tbsps *mirin*
2 Tbsps sugar
3 Tbsps dark soy sauce

Cut the chicken legs apart at the joint. Drop into boiling water until the color changes. Transfer immediately to cold water and drain.

Combine the chicken, kelp, and water for simmering in a soup pot. Cover with a drop-lid (page 143) and place over high heat. Just before the water boils, remove and discard the kelp. Bring to a boil and reduce heat to low. Simmer until the liquid is reduced to about a third of its original volume (about 1 hour).

Add the saké, *mirin*, and sugar. Simmer for 5 more minutes and add the soy sauce. Simmer for a final 5 minutes, remove from heat, and let the chicken cool in the liquid.

Cut the long onions (or scallions) into 1-inch (3-cm) lengths. Grill the long onions on a wire net over a gas flame until the surface scorches slightly. (If using scallions, grilling is unnecessary.)

String the snow peas and boil in lightly salted water until just tender (about 1 minute). Refresh in cold water and drain.

When the chicken has cooled or you are ready to serve (whichever is later), remove it from the simmering liquid and bone. Discard the bones and return chicken to the pot. Reheat over high heat and boil, occasionally ladling liquid over chicken, until the liquid is reduced by about half.

Add the onion and snow peas and quickly heat through.

Arrange the chicken and vegetables in dishes, add some sauce, sprinkle with pepper, and serve.

674 Cals

Remove bones from cooked chicken

62

Chicken Escabeche Nanban

Toriniku nanban-zuke

The term nanban, *or "Southern barbarians," refers to the foreigners who came to Japan before the country was closed at the beginning of the seventeenth century, but especially to the Spanish and Portuguese missionaries and traders who shocked the Japanese with their taste for bizarre victuals. Today, dishes with red chili peppers—unknown in Japan until their importation for use in the foreign community of several centuries past—still receive this dubious appellation.*

In this recipe, the vinegar marinade, with its seasoning of chili peppers and grilled onions, softens the odor and reduces the oiliness of the chicken, giving it a lighter, more refreshing taste. The key point is to place the deep-fried chicken (it can also be grilled) in the marinade while the meat is still hot. Once the sauce has had a chance to soak into the chicken—a few minutes—the food is ready, but it will be even tastier after marinating for a day or so, making this an ideal dish for a party. Apple or other fruit vinegars substituted for the rice vinegar will produce interesting variations.

Serves 4

vegetable oil for deep-frying
1 lb (450 g) boned chicken thighs
flour

MARINADE

1 white long onion or 2–3 scallions
1 medium onion
1 Tbsp vegetable oil
2–3 dried red chili peppers
¾ cup (180 ml) rice vinegar
¾ cup (180 ml) bonito stock (*dashi*) (page 140)
3 Tbsps sugar
2 Tbsps light soy sauce
1 Tbsp dark soy sauce

Make the MARINADE: Cut the long onion (or scallions) into 1-inch (3-cm) lengths. Grill on a wire net over a gas flame until slightly scorched (or sauté in a frying pan until soft). Slice the round onion thinly. Heat the vegetable oil in a frying pan, add the onion, and sauté over high heat until it becomes soft and transparent. Remove the stems and seeds from the chili peppers. Combine the remaining ingredients in a saucepan, add the long onion (or scallion), onion, and chili peppers, and bring to a boil over high heat. Remove from heat and let cool.

Preheat the vegetable oil to a low deep-frying temperature (330° F/165° C).

Cut any ligaments, then cut the chicken into 1-inch (3-cm) squares. Dredge in flour. Deep-fry until golden brown.

While the chicken is still hot, place it in the marinade. Set aside for several minutes to allow marinade to soak in, or marinate, covered and unrefrigerated, for 24 hours to allow flavor to fully mature.

Retrieve the red pepper from the marinade and slice into thin rounds. Arrange the chicken on serving plates, garnish with long onion (or scallion) and onion, spoon on marinade, and top with red pepper rounds. Serve hot or warm from the marinade or at room temperature.

417 Cals

Soak deep-fried chicken at least 5 minutes in marinade or marinate 24 hours for best flavor

Tatsuta Fried Chicken

Toriniku tatsuta-age

Red maple leaves are the symbol of fall in Japan, and a pilgrimage to one of the famous maple-viewing spots is almost mandatory. The Tatsuta River, near Nara, has a long history as one of the most famous places to celebrate fall and the changing colors. This dish takes its name from this scenic river, for when chicken is marinated in soy sauce and deep-fried it takes on a color reminiscent of autumn maple leaves. Serve it in the fall for a uniquely Japanese mood.

Serves 4

1 lb (450 g) boned chicken thighs
vegetable oil for deep-frying
1 sweet red pepper
1 bell pepper
cornstarch
4 lemon wedges

SEASONING

2 Tbsps dark soy sauce
2 Tbsps saké
1 tsp fresh ginger juice (page 145)

COATING

2 egg whites
2–3 Tbsps cornstarch
2 Tbsps finely chopped and rinsed scallion
1 Tbsp finely chopped fresh ginger

Cut the chicken into 1-inch (3-cm) squares about ¼ inch (¾ cm) thick. Combine the SEASONING ingredients and marinate the chicken for 20–30 minutes.

Preheat the oil to a low deep-frying temperature (330° F/165° C).

Core and seed the peppers. Use small cookie cutters to cut the peppers into decorative shapes—maple leaves are traditional, but any shape will do.

Make the COATING: Beat the egg whites until they are frothy but not stiff, then add the cornstarch and mix well. Add the scallion and ginger.

Dredge the chicken in cornstarch and then cover well with coating mixture. Deep-fry the chicken. Do not overcook. It should fry gently; when it stops bubbling vigorously and before it becomes too brown, remove from the oil.

Deep-fry the pepper shapes until their surface is tender—this will require only 30 seconds at most. Be careful not to overcook them. Remove and sprinkle with salt.

Arrange the chicken and pepper on serving plates, garnish with a lemon wedge, and serve.

516 Cals

After dredging chicken in cornstarch, cover well with egg-white coating

Chicken, Grapefruit, and Corn Salad with Almond Dressing

Toriniku, gurepufurutsu, mashu no amondo-ae

In Japan, salad dressings based on sesame are extremely popular. Here is a variation that plays upon almonds to create a similar, but more Western, effect. The ingredients for the salad itself are also familiar to Americans: grapefruit, chicken, and corn salad. Try kiwi fruit or avocado for grapefruit, or any green leafy vegetable for corn salad.

Serves 4

10 oz (300 g) chicken breast
sections from ½ grapefruit
2 oz (60 g) corn salad

ALMOND DRESSING
¾ cup (120 g) shelled whole almonds, with skin
⅔ cup (160 ml) bonito stock (*dashi*) (page 140)
7 Tbsps rice vinegar
4 Tbsps dark soy sauce
2 Tbsps sugar

Soak the almonds for the dressing in boiling water for 2 minutes, plunge into cold water, drain, and remove the skins with your fingers. Pat dry. Place the almonds in a dry frying pan and parch over low heat until golden brown—about 15 minutes—or toast them in a 360° F (180° C) oven for 30 minutes.

Boil the chicken breast in lightly salted water until done. Remove from heat and let the chicken cool in the water.

Make the ALMOND DRESSING: Place the almonds in a food processor and whir to a rough paste, add the remaining ingredients, and whir to a smooth paste. Force through a fine drum sieve.

Seed the grapefruit sections, remove the section skin, and slice each section lengthwise into 2 identical halves.

Separate the corn salad leaves. Cut the larger ones into 2–3 pieces so that all the leaves are fairly uniform in size.

Drain and shred the chicken.

Spread out the dressing on serving plates and arrange the chicken, grapefruit, and corn salad on top (or combine all the ingredients with the dressing, then toss). Serve.

272 Cals

Egg

Savory Custard Cup

Chawan-mushi

This is a representative Japanese egg dish in which the egg, the soup stock, and the other ingredients are savored as a whole. The secret is to use as much stock as possible in proportion to the eggs: the custard should set, but just barely, giving a gentle, almost liquid, sensation when eaten. This dish is usually served piping hot, but it is also excellent chilled in the summer.

Serves 4

3 oz (90 g) spinach

4 oz (120 g) boned chicken thigh

1 tsp saké

1 tsp light soy sauce

4 raw shrimp, 1 oz (25 g) each, shelled and deveined (page 48)

4 fresh shiitake mushrooms, washed and stems removed, or 4 fresh brown mushrooms, washed and trimmed

4 tsps fresh ginger juice (page 145)

CUSTARD

2½ cups (600 ml) bonito stock (*dashi*) (page 140)

1 Tbsp light soy sauce

1 tsp *mirin*

½ tsp salt

3 eggs

TO PREPARE

Parboil the spinach in lightly salted water, drain, and refresh in cold water for 10 minutes. Drain again and wring out any excess water. Cut the spinach into 1-inch (3-cm) lengths.

Cut the chicken into ½-inch (1-cm) squares and sprinkle with the saké and soy sauce.

Drop the shrimp in boiling water for a few seconds until they change color. Refresh in cold water, drain, pat dry, and quarter crosswise.

Quarter the mushroom caps.

TO MAKE

Make the CUSTARD: Heat the bonito stock, then season with the soy sauce, *mirin*, and salt. Bring to a boil over high heat, remove from heat, and let cool to room temperature. Beat the eggs lightly, add the seasoned stock, and strain mixture through gauze.

Preheat a steamer over high heat.

Divide the chicken, shrimp, mushroom, and spinach among 4 custard cups with lids (or use heat-resistant coffee cups and saucers or foil). Pour in the custard and cover

with lid (or foil or small saucers) to keep condensed moisture from dripping onto custard.

Place the covered cups in the preheated steamer over high heat. When the surface turns white (about 3–5 minutes), reduce heat to medium-low and steam for 15 minutes.

Test the custard by inserting a bamboo skewer or toothpick well into the center of one cup. The custard is done when the liquid flowing from the puncture runs clear. The surface of the finished custard should be moist and slick (not cracked and parched). Uncover, spoon 1 tsp of ginger juice into each cup, place on a saucer, and serve hot or chilled in the cup.

155 Cals

Strain custard through gauze

Divide solid ingredients among 4 cups, then ladle in custard

If liquid from hole runs clear, custard is done

Wrapped Custard

Fukusa tamago

In this attractive dish, shrimp and snippets of vegetables add color to seasoned egg, which is then wrapped in plastic and boiled until it "sets." Any number of variations can be created by substituting white-fleshed fish, sea urchin, or chicken for the shrimp, or by changing the "palette" of vegetables—simply be sure to avoid ingredients with pungent odors. Here the custard is served cold, but you may prefer to eat it hot, topped with steaming sauce. It can be added to soups or coated with flour and deep-fried.

Serves 4

1 dried cloud ear mushroom
4 raw shrimp, 1 oz (25 g) each, shelled and deveined (page 48)
8 green beans
⅛ medium carrot
mint leaves

CUSTARD

4 eggs, beaten
4½ Tbsps bonito stock (*dashi*) (page 140)
1 tsp *mirin*
¼ tsp salt

SAUCE

1¼ cups (300 ml) bonito stock (*dashi*) (page 140)
2 Tbsps saké
2 tsps *mirin*
1 tsp light soy sauce
scant ¼ tsp salt
1 Tbsp cornstarch dissolved in 1 Tbsp water
1 tsp fresh ginger juice (page 145)

Soak the mushroom for about 1 hour (page 142), cut into ¼-inch (½-cm) squares, and parboil in lightly salted water.

Parboil the shrimp just until the surface turns light pink. Immediately drop into cold water, then drain and quarter.

Cut the green beans and carrot into ¼-inch (½-cm) pieces, parboil separately in lightly salted water, plunge into cold water, and drain.

Pour egg mixture into cup lined with plastic wrap, then close plastic and tie

Boil pouches for 10 minutes

Combine all the CUSTARD ingredients. Strain through gauze.

Line 4 teacups with plastic wrap. Divide the shrimp and vegetables among the cups, and pour one-fourth of the egg mixture into each. Bring up the ends of the plastic wrap and tie with kitchen string. Drop the plastic pouches in very hot water kept just below the boiling point. Cook for 10 minutes.

Plunge the custard—pouch and all—into cold water to cool, then into ice water to chill.

Combine all the SAUCE ingredients, except the cornstarch and ginger juice, in a saucepan and bring to a boil. Blend the cornstarch dissolved in water into the stock until it thickens. Add the ginger juice, bring the sauce back just to the boiling point, and cool the saucepan in cold water, then in ice water.

Unwrap each package, arrange in individual serving dishes, spoon in some sauce, and garnish with mint leaves.

139 Cals

Japanese Coddled Egg
Ondo tamago

With this egg dish, the combination of consistencies is everything: the rich custardlike body of the yolk proves just the right counterpoint to the light half-fluid of the white. Said to have been discovered quite accidentally when someone tried to cook eggs in the thermal waters of a hot spring, this cooking method takes advantage of the curious fact that yolk and white solidify at different temperatures. Success depends, then, on keeping the heat constant. Eaten cold—as here—or hot, this egg dish, with its subtle texture, is bound to find a place in your repertoire.

Serves 4

4 eggs
1 cup (240 ml) bonito stock (*dashi*) (page 140)
3 Tbsps light soy sauce
3 Tbsps *mirin*

¼ cup loose bonito flakes (⅙ oz/5 g)
2 pods okra
wasabi horseradish

kitchen thermometer

Heat ample water to 152°–154° F (67°–68° C) and adjust the heat or add cold water as necessary to maintain a constant temperature. Place the eggs in the heated water and cook for 25 minutes, keeping an eye on the thermometer.

Crack one egg to test. If done, the egg white will be soft and just set, the egg yolk soft cooked. Cool the eggs in cold water, then chill in ice water.

Prepare the sauce by combining bonito stock, soy sauce, and *mirin* in a saucepan. Bring to a boil, then add the bonito flakes. Remove from the heat, immediately strain to clarify (page 142), and chill.

Trim okra caps and dredge pods in salt. Rub with a scouring motion to remove tiny hairs. Boil until just tender, then transfer to cold water, cool, drain, and slice thinly.

Crack eggs into chilled individual bowls. Spoon in some sauce, garnish with sliced okra, top with *wasabi* horseradish, and serve.

106 Cals

Tofu

Simmered Tofu

Yudofu

This is the tofu dish par excellence, highly prized throughout Japan from Buddhist monasteries to humble drinking establishments. Simmered Tofu is so much a symbol of winter in Japan that its name has become a "season word" in haiku.

Simmered in a light kelp stock, and served with only light condiments, it is an extremely simple dish, but precisely for that reason, the taste and texture of the tofu itself is in the spotlight. The secret is in the timing: for the best flavor, the tofu should be eaten as soon as the heat of the stock has penetrated to the center of each cube—a moment longer and the soft, luxurious texture will have been lost. In order to catch the tofu at the right moment, this dish is best cooked at the table where the tender tofu can be plucked from the steaming pot as soon as it is ready.

Serves 4

2-inch (5-cm) length kelp (*konbu*)

2 blocks tofu, about 20 oz (600 g) total

DIPPING SAUCE

1 cup (240 ml) bonito stock (*dashi*) (page 140)

½ cup (120 ml) dark soy sauce

2 Tbsps saké

2 Tbsps *mirin*

¼ cup loose bonito flakes (⅙ oz/5 g)

CONDIMENTS

2 scallions

1 sheet *nori* seaweed

2 Tbsps white sesame seeds

2 Tbsps finely grated fresh ginger

½ cup loose bonito threads or flakes (⅓ oz/10 g)

Chop the scallions finely, wrap in cheesecloth, and wash well under cold running water. Squeeze out as much water as possible. Separate scallion pieces if clumped together.

Toast the *nori* seaweed over a high gas flame (if it has not been pretoasted), then crumble (page 143).

Toast the sesame seeds (page 140) and chop coarsely on a dry cloth.

Make the DIPPING SAUCE: Combine the bonito stock, soy sauce, saké, and *mirin* in a saucepan and bring to a boil over high heat. Add the bonito flakes, remove from heat immediately, and strain to clarify (page 142).

Fill a large pot or a deep electric skillet to the halfway point with cold water and add the *konbu* kelp. Heat over medium heat. Cut each block of tofu into 8 pieces and simmer in hot (not boiling) water.

Reheat the sauce and serve in individual bowls (or place it in a heatproof container and position in the center of the tofu pot—the traditional method).

When the tofu floats, it is ready to be eaten. Season the individual bowls of dipping sauce with condiments as desired (or let each diner remove a piece of tofu to his or her serving bowl, top with sauce from the center of the pot, and season with condiments).

170 Cals

Cut tofu block into 8 pieces

Night-Dried Tofu with Chicken Sauce

Ichiya-dofu tori soboro an-kake

Night-Dried Tofu takes its name from the fact that the tofu is allowed to freeze overnight. This gives the tofu a different texture and a more "condensed" taste. Once the tofu has been simmered, it is cooled in the pot liquid, allowing the seasoning to penetrate throughout. The chicken sauce enhances the richness and texture of the dish, and spinach adds color (substitute snow peas or green beans). Tofu dried overnight can also be used in miso soup or one-pot dishes, or deep-fried and smothered with Amber Sauce (page 75).

Serves 4

1 block regular ("cotton") tofu, about 10 oz (300 g)

1 Tbsp vegetable oil

4 oz (120 g) ground chicken

10 oz (300 g) spinach

3 Tbsps cornstarch dissolved in 3 Tbsps water

2 Tbsps fresh ginger juice (page 145)

FOR SIMMERING

2 cups (480 ml) bonito stock (*dashi*) (page 140)

3 Tbsps dark soy sauce

3 Tbsps saké

3 Tbsps *mirin*

1 Tbsp sugar

SEASONING FOR CHICKEN

2 tsps dark soy sauce

2 tsps saké

2 tsps *mirin*

2 tsps fresh ginger juice (page 145)

TO PREPARE

Remove any packaging from the tofu, rinse, wrap in cheesecloth, and freeze overnight.

TO MAKE

Bring an ample amount of water to a boil in a saucepan over high heat. Add the (unwrapped) frozen tofu and boil for 7 minutes. Drain and cut into 8 pieces.

Combine the SIMMERING ingredients in a saucepan and bring to a boil over high heat. Add the tofu, then cover with a drop-lid (page 143). When the liquid returns to a boil, reduce the heat to low and simmer for 10 minutes. Remove from heat and let cool in the simmering liquid.

Heat the vegetable oil in a frying pan over high heat, add the ground chicken and sauté until the meat separates and becomes crumbly. Add the SEASONING ingredients and continue stir-frying until the liquid is nearly gone. Turn the chicken out into a strainer or colander and let drain and cool.

Boil the spinach in lightly salted water until just tender, then refresh in cold water and drain. Remove some simmering liquid from the tofu, cool, and then soak the spinach in it.

When you are ready to serve, reheat the tofu and spinach (separately) in the simmering liquid. Wring the spinach, then cut into 1-inch (3-cm) lengths. Arrange the tofu and spinach in serving bowls.

Strain the remaining pot liquid to clarify (page 142). Combine the chicken and pot liquid over high heat and bring to a boil, thicken with the cornstarch dissolved in water, then gently stir in the ginger juice. Bring to a boil, remove immediately from heat, and spoon over the tofu.

261 Cals

Night-dried tofu (above) and untreated tofu

Simmered Tofu Dumplings

Ganmodoki uma-ni

The Japanese name for this dish, Ganmo-doki, means "like a wild goose," and it is said that these succulent golden dumplings, made by mixing ground tofu with vegetables and shrimp, are similar in flavor and appearance to the traditional cuisine associated with the wild goose, a favorite Japanese symbol of the passing of the seasons. Ganmodoki tofu dumplings are a rare delicacy even when served immediately with a light bonito stock seasoned with ginger, but here they are sim-mered slowly in a much richer sauce. The shrimp can be replaced with scallops or white-fleshed fish, and the addition of crab or other shellfish make it an even rarer treat.

Weighting and draining wrapped tofu (here tofu is partially exposed)

Whir dumpling ingredients to a smooth paste

Mix in mushroom and carrot

Slide dumplings into oil

Douse deep-fried dumplings with boiling water

Add soy sauce and simmer a final 5 minutes

Serves 4

vegetable oil for deep-frying
8 pods okra
1 zucchini, about ½ lb (220 g)
2 tsps finely grated ginger

DUMPLINGS

1½ blocks regular ("cotton") tofu, about
   15 oz (450 g) total
2 dried cloud ear mushrooms
¼ medium carrot
10 oz (300 g) raw shrimp, shelled and
   deveined (page 48)
1 egg, lightly beaten
⅓ tsp salt
4 tsps *mirin*
1 Tbsp light soy sauce
2 tsps sugar

FOR SIMMERING

2½ cups (600 ml) bonito stock (*dashi*) (page
   140)
4½ Tbsps *mirin*
1 Tbsp sugar
2½ Tbsps dark soy sauce

TO PREPARE

Wrap the tofu in cheesecloth or a clean kitchen cloth and sandwich between 2 cutting boards. Incline one end of the cutting boards to facilitate draining, weight down the tofu with a bowl partially filled with water (1 cup [240 ml] water equals ½ lb [220 g]; the combined weight should total about 1 lb [450 g]), and allow tofu to drain for 1½–2 hours.

Soak the mushrooms for 1 hour (page 142).

TO MAKE

Preheat the oil to a low deep-frying temperature (320° F/160° C).

Finely dice the mushrooms and carrots. Parboil separately in lightly salted water, then refresh in cold water and drain.

Combine all the DUMPLING ingredients in a food processor, except the diced mushroom and carrot, and whir to a smooth paste (or mince the shrimp, force the tofu and shrimp through a fine drum sieve, grind in a mortar and pestle, then add the remaining ingredients—except the mushroom and carrot—in order and one at a time, grinding as you go).

Remove the dumpling mixture to a bowl, add the diced mushroom and carrot, and mix well.

Form the tofu mixture into small balls about 1 inch (3 cm) in diameter and deep-fry to a golden brown.

Place the dumplings in a colander and pour boiling water over them to remove any excess oil.

Combine the dumplings and bonito stock in a saucepan, cover with a drop-lid (page 143), and bring to a boil over high heat. Reduce heat to low and simmer for 5 minutes. Add the *mirin* and sugar, then simmer for 5 more minutes. Add the soy sauce and simmer for a final 5 minutes. Set aside in saucepan and let cool.

Trim the okra caps and dredge the pods in salt. Rub in a scouring motion to remove the tiny hairs. Boil in salted water until just tender, then refresh in cold water. Soak in several tablespoons of cooled simmering liquid from the dumplings.

Peel the zucchini, cut lengthwise into 4–6 strips, then into 2-inch (5-cm) pieces. Boil in salted water until just tender, refresh in cold water, then soak in several tablespoons of cooled simmering liquid from the dumplings.

Reheat the dumplings, okra, and zucchini separately in the simmering liquid they are standing in. Arrange in serving bowls, add some sauce, and top with grated ginger.

265 Cals

Deep-Fried Tofu

Agedashi-dofu

The light flavor of tofu adapts to almost any cooking method, but it is particularly susceptible to deep-frying. The tofu cubes turn a crispy golden brown on the outside, while the center is heated yet retains its distinctive texture—if it is skillfully prepared. Wrapping the tofu in cheesecloth reduces the moisture content somewhat; the key is to leave some of the moisture in the drained tofu to ensure that the finished dish is neither too hard nor too soft. Though here it is served with a thick sauce, deep-fried tofu can also be added to soups or simmered dishes.

Serves 4

1 block tofu, about 10 oz (300 g)
vegetable oil for deep-frying
flour

AMBER SAUCE

1 ¼ cups (300 ml) bonito stock (*dashi*) (page 140)
5 Tbsps dark soy sauce
5 Tbsps *mirin*
¼ cup loose bonito flakes (⅙ oz/5 g)
3 Tbsps cornstarch dissolved in 3 Tbsps water
1 Tbsp fresh ginger juice (page 145)

CONDIMENTS

½ cup loose bonito threads or flakes (⅓ oz/10 g)
1 Tbsp finely grated fresh ginger
3 Tbsps finely chopped and rinsed scallion

TO PREPARE

Wrap the tofu in cheesecloth or a clean kitchen cloth and set aside to drain for 1½–2 hours. Draining time may be reduced by 30 minutes if using regular ("cotton") tofu.

TO MAKE

Preheat the oil to a low deep-frying temperature (330° F/165° C).

Quarter the tofu and coat with flour.

Deep-fry the tofu until it turns a light brown. Remove from the oil and drain on absorbent paper.

Make the AMBER SAUCE: Combine the bonito stock, soy sauce, and *mirin* in a saucepan. Bring to a boil over high heat, add the bonito flakes, and immediately remove from heat. Strain to clarify (page 142). Return the sauce to the pan and heat again. When it boils, thicken with the cornstarch dissolved in water, add the ginger juice, return to a boil, and remove from heat.

To serve, arrange the tofu in serving bowls and add several tablespoons of the sauce. Top with bonito threads or flakes and stack grated ginger and chopped scallions alongside or allow diners to season with condiments to taste.

145 Cals

Scrambled Tofu

Iri-dofu

Extremely easy to prepare, this dish has long been a favorite. Stir-frying reduces the moisture in the tofu and allows it to absorb the flavors of the other ingredients, so the more vigorously you stir, and the more crumbled the tofu becomes, the better. The eggs stirred in at the end are for texture, and they should be moist, not hard, when the dish is served. The chicken skin is used for its robustness but it can be replaced with fattier substitutes such as thin deep-fried tofu (usuage) or pork.

Serves 4

1 block regular ("cotton") tofu, about 10 oz (300 g)

4 dried cloud ear mushrooms

2 oz (60 g) chicken skin

½ medium carrot

2 oz (60 g) snow peas (about 20)

2 Tbsps vegetable oil

2 eggs

FOR SIMMERING

½ cup (120 ml) bonito stock (*dashi*) (page 140)

3 Tbsps sugar

2 Tbsps light soy sauce

½ tsp salt

TO PREPARE

Press moisture from the tofu for 1½–2 hours (page 74).

Soak the mushrooms for 1 hour (page 142).

TO MAKE

Cut the chicken skin into ½-inch (1-cm) squares.

Cut the carrot and mushroom into 2-inch (5-cm) slivers. Boil each vegetable separately in lightly salted water for 1–2 minutes, then refresh in cold water and drain. Boil the snow peas in lightly salted water until just tender. Refresh, drain, and cut crosswise into julienne strips, discarding any peas that fall out of the pods.

Heat the vegetable oil in a pan, add the chicken skin, and stir-fry briefly over medium heat until the surface becomes crispy. Crumble the tofu into coarse chunks, add to the pan, and stir-fry well. Add the carrot and mushroom and continue to stir-fry over medium heat.

When the mixture becomes dry, add the SIMMERING ingredients. Simmer until the liquid is almost completely reduced.

Add the lightly beaten egg and stir gently. When the egg sets but is still moist, add the snow peas, stir once, and remove from heat.

Transfer to warmed serving plates.

295 Cals

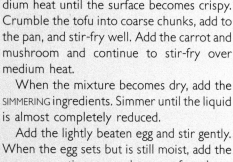

Add tofu and stir-fry

Add egg and cook until just set

76

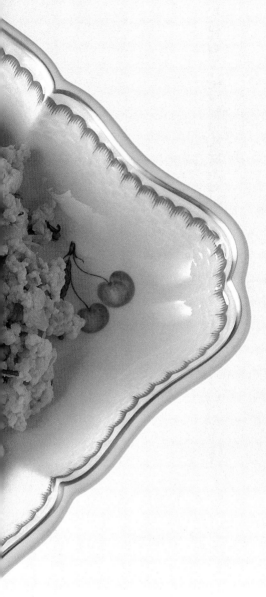

White Salad

Shira-ae

This is a light dressing, so the distinctive flavor of the simmered shiitake mushrooms is indispensable and pulls everything together. Besides chicken, other ingredients such as thin deep-fried tofu (usuage), seasoned konnyaku, cooked mushrooms, or simmered carrots can be added.

Serves 4

3 dried shiitake mushrooms

1 cucumber

1 chicken breast, boned and skinned, about ½ lb (220 g)

FOR SIMMERING MUSHROOMS

⅔ cup (150 ml) bonito stock (*dashi*) (page 140)

3½ Tbsps water from soaking shiitake mushrooms (see To Prepare)

2 Tbsps sugar

1 Tbsp *mirin*

2 Tbsps dark soy sauce

TOFU DRESSING

½ block regular ("cotton") tofu, about 5 oz (150 g)

3 Tbsps bonito stock (*dashi*) (page 140)

1 Tbsp sesame paste (page 140)

1½ tsps sugar

¼ tsp salt

dash light soy sauce

TO PREPARE

Soak the shiitake mushrooms for 6–7 hours (page 142). Reserve water.

Press out moisture from the tofu for 1½–2 hours (page 74).

TO MAKE

Remove the mushrooms and strain the shiitake soaking liquid to clarify (page 142).

Simmer the mushrooms: Combine the bonito stock and shiitake soaking liquid in a saucepan, add the mushrooms, cover with a drop-lid (page 143), and bring to a boil over high heat. Reduce heat to low and simmer for 10 minutes. Add the sugar and *mirin* and simmer for another 5 minutes. Add the soy sauce and simmer until the liquid has been almost completely reduced.

Peel the cucumber, then quarter. Scrape out the seeds. Slice the cucumber thinly, then soak in salted water (1½ tsps salt to 1 cup [240 ml] water) for 20 minutes to tenderize. Drain and wring out excess water with your hands.

Boil the chicken breast in lightly salted water until it is cooked through. Cut into ⅛ × ⅛ × 1-inch (¼ × ¼ × 3-cm) strips.

Cut the simmered mushrooms into thin strips.

Combine all the TOFU DRESSING ingredients in a food processor and mix to a smooth paste (or force the tofu through a fine drum sieve, combine remaining dressing ingredients with tofu). Force paste through a sieve.

Squeeze any excess water from the mushroom and cucumber. Toss all the ingredients with the dressing. Serve.

173 Cals

Tofu Sandwiches

Tofu hakata-ni

Hakata is an area of Japan famous for its striped kimono-sash (obi) material, and it is this striped pattern that gives this dish its Japanese name. It requires a bit of extra effort, but the dedicated cook will be delighted with the results. When steaming and simmering, watch the heat: keep it fairly low, since cooking over higher heats will cause the layers to separate. For a provocative variation, substitute freeze-dried tofu (Koyadofu) for regular tofu.

Serves 4

1⅓ blocks regular ("cotton") tofu (see To Prepare)
cornstarch

¾ cup (100 g) shelled green peas
¼ lb (120 g) spinach

SHRIMP FILLING

14 oz (400 g) raw shrimp, shelled and deveined (page 48)
1 egg yolk
pinch salt
1 Tbsp saké
¼ tsp *mirin*
1 tsp fresh ginger juice (page 145)
1 Tbsp cornstarch dissolved in 1 Tbsp water

SIMMERING

3⅓ cups (800 ml) bonito stock (*dashi*) (page 140)
4 Tbsps sugar
3½ Tbsps light soy sauce
3 Tbsps *mirin*

TO PREPARE

This recipe yields 4 triple-deck sandwiches, the ⅓ block (cut it crosswise from a whole block) making the fourth sandwich. Press moisture from the tofu for 1½–2 hours (page 74).

TO MAKE

Combine all the SHRIMP FILLING ingredients in a food processor and whir to a fine paste (or chop the shrimp, grind in a mortar and pestle, and then add the remaining ingredients in order and one by one, grinding as you go). Force through a fine drum sieve.

Cut the whole block of tofu crosswise into thirds (with the extra ⅓ block, you should have 4 equal pieces). Then slice each block horizontally into thirds—slices will be approximately ¼ inch (½ cm) thick.

Spread out the 12 tofu slices and sprinkle 8 of them lightly with cornstarch. Cover the

8 slices with the filling, spreading it to the edges. Sprinkle the filling with cornstarch.

Now build 4 triple-deck sandwiches— 3 slices of tofu filled with 2 layers of shrimp paste. Carefully remove any excess filling from the edges.

Preheat a steamer over medium-high heat.

Wrap each sandwich separately in a small (6 × 8-inch/15 × 20-cm) piece of gauze. Steam for 15 minutes.

Combine the SIMMERING ingredients in a saucepan and bring to a boil over high heat. Reduce the heat to low, add the tofu sandwiches (still in their wrappers) to the simmering liquid, cover with a drop-lid (page 143), and simmer for 10 minutes. Remove pan from heat and let tofu cool in the liquid.

Sprinkle the green peas with salt, rub gently, then drop in boiling water, cover with a drop-lid, and cook until just tender. Remove the pan from heat and gradually add cold water to cool. Drain. Transfer ½ cup (120 ml) of cooled simmering liquid to a separate pan and soak the peas in it.

Boil the spinach in lightly salted water until just tender. Refresh in cold water, then drain and wring out any excess water.

TO SERVE

Reheat the tofu sandwiches in the simmering liquid, then remove and unwrap. Slice each sandwich into thirds and arrange in serving bowls. Strain the remaining simmering liquid to clarify (page 142) and heat in a saucepan over high heat. Soak the spinach in the liquid to warm, then drain and cut into 1½-inch (4-cm) lengths. Arrange the spinach next to the tofu. Warm the green peas in their soaking liquid.

Spoon several tablespoons of the pot liquid over the tofu and spinach. Drain the green peas and sprinkle over the sandwiches.

274 Cals

Whir filling to a fine paste

Press through a fine drum sieve

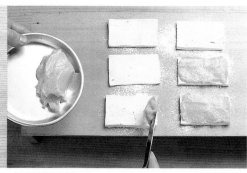
Cut each of the 4 pieces horizontally into thirds

Sprinkle with cornstarch, spread on filling, and sprinkle filling with cornstarch

Build 4 triple-deck tofu sandwiches

Wrap sandwiches in gauze

Steam

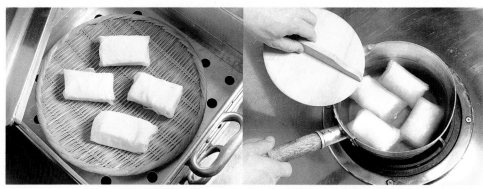
Simmer wrapped sandwiches with drop-lid

Tofu Hamburger Steak

This variation on tofu cuisine takes its cue from hamburger steak. Well-drained tofu is pureed and mixed with miso, chopped mushroom, and scallion, then made into patties and pan-fried in the same way as hamburger steak. Here a basic tomato sauce with a little soy sauce for a Japanese touch is used. Tofu has gained great popularity as a healthfood, and this is an excellent recipe for the cook who wishes to introduce tofu into the daily diet.

Serves 4

2 blocks regular ("cotton") tofu, about 10 oz (300 g) each
6 dried cloud ear mushrooms
1 potato
1 medium carrot
1 Tbsp nonsweet white miso paste
⅓ tsp salt
1 egg, lightly beaten
2 scallions, finely chopped and rinsed
flour
2 Tbsps vegetable oil
1 Tbsp butter
4 sprigs watercress

SAUCE

1 Tbsp vegetable oil
½ onion, finely chopped
1 medium-sized ripe tomato, peeled, seeded, and coarsely chopped
½ cup (120 ml) tomato puree
1 cup (240 ml) chicken stock (page 22)
2½ Tbsps dark soy sauce
pepper

TO PREPARE

Press the water from the tofu for 1 hour (page 74).

Soften the mushrooms in water for 1 hour (page 142).

Peel the potato and carrot, cut into bite-sized pieces, and soak in cold water (separately) until ready to use.

TO MAKE

Chop the mushrooms finely, parboil in boiling water, refresh in cold water, then drain well.

Whir the tofu in a food processor (or force through a fine drum sieve and grind in a mortar and pestle). Add the miso, salt, and lightly beaten egg and mix well (or add one at a time to mortar). Add the scallion and mushroom and mix gently.

Form the tofu mixture into 4 patties and coat lightly with flour.

Heat the oil and butter together in a frying pan over medium heat, add the patties, reduce heat to medium-low, and fry until lightly browned. Turn and brown the other side. Total cooking time should be about 10 minutes.

Make the SAUCE while the tofu burgers are frying. Heat the vegetable oil in a saucepan over medium-low heat, add the onion, and sauté until lightly browned. Add the tomato and stir gently, then add the tomato puree and chicken stock. Adjust the seasoning with soy sauce and pepper. Bring to a boil, then remove from heat. Transfer to a blender (let cool slightly if your machine cannot accept very hot liquids) and whir until smooth.

Prepare the vegetables. Parboil the potato and carrot separately in lightly salted water, then drain. Heat butter in a frying pan over medium heat, add the potato and carrot, and sauté briefly. Season with salt and pepper.

Spoon the sauce onto warmed plates, set the tofu burgers on the bed of sauce, add the potato and carrot, garnish with a sprig of watercress, and serve.

276 Cals

Freeze-Dried Tofu with Egg
Koya-dofu tama-jime

Freeze-dried tofu, originally made by leaving tofu out in the winter cold to freeze and dehydrate naturally, was an important protein food in the diet of vegetarian Buddhist priests—the Japanese name Koya-dofu comes from the monastic center on Mt. Koya. Today's factory-made freeze-dried tofu differs somewhat from the natural product of old, but is easier to use. Most important, however, are the preparatory steps for reconstituting the tofu; be sure to soak the tofu in water no hotter than 180° F (80° C) and to thoroughly press out all cloudy liquid.

Serves 4

4 cakes freeze-dried tofu (*Koya-dofu*), about 2½ oz (70 g) total

1 head broccoli, about ½ lb (220 g)

3 eggs, lightly beaten

FOR SIMMERING

2½ cups (600 ml) bonito stock (*dashi*) (page 140)

3½ Tbsps light soy sauce

3 Tbsps sugar

5 tsps *mirin*

1 tsp salt

TO PREPARE

Place the freeze-dried tofu in hot (about 180° F/80° C) water, cover with a drop-lid (page 143), and let stand for 5 minutes to reconstitute, turning once halfway through the soaking time.

Gently press the tofu between the palms of your hands to squeeze out water. Release, allow the tofu to expand in a bowl of clean tap water, and press again. Continue until water pressed from the tofu runs clear, then squeeze out any remaining water.

Cut each cake into 6 pieces. Combine the SIMMERING ingredients in a saucepan, add the tofu, cover with a drop-lid, and bring to a boil over high heat. Reduce the heat to low and simmer for 10 minutes. Remove from heat let the tofu cool in the broth for 2–3 hours to absorb the flavors.

TO MAKE

Cut the broccoli into small florets and boil for 3 minutes in lightly salted water until just tender. Refresh in cold water and drain.

Reheat the tofu in the simmering liquid, add the broccoli, and bring to a boil. Add the lightly beaten egg in a circular motion to cover as much of the surface as possible, cover with a drop-lid, and remove from heat. Let the egg set in the pan for 2–3 minutes.

Ladle the tofu and egg along with some broth into bowls and serve.

212 Cals

Press reconstituted tofu until water is no longer milky

Cover whole surface with egg

Vegetables

Stuffed Potato Buns

Jagaimo manju

Tender shrimp blanketed in a smooth potato dough and topped with hot Silver Sauce make a truly beautiful and satisfying winter meal. What's more, these buns can be prepared in advance and steamed at the last minute, making it a perfect party dish. You won't want to limit yourself to potatoes and shrimp; this recipe works just as well for, say, pumpkin buns stuffed with chicken, pork, beef, white-fleshed fish, or crab.

Serves 4

POTATO BUNS

2 medium potatoes, 6–7 oz (180–200 g) each

pinch salt

1 Tbsp butter

1 egg white, lightly beaten

3 Tbsps cornstarch

SHRIMP STUFFING

10 oz (300 g) raw shrimp, shelled and deveined (page 48)

1 Tbsp saké

1 Tbsp *mirin*

2 tsps light soy sauce

SPINACH

½ lb (220 g) spinach

1 cup (240 ml) bonito stock (*dashi*) (page 140)

2 Tbsps light soy sauce

2 Tbsps *mirin*

SILVER SAUCE

1⅔ cups (400 ml) bonito stock (*dashi*) (page 140)

2 Tbsps light soy sauce

4 tsps *mirin*

pinch salt

3 Tbsps cornstarch dissolved in 3 Tbsps water

1 Tbsp fresh ginger juice (page 145)

2 Tbsps finely grated fresh ginger

Begin the POTATO BUNS: Peel the potatoes, chop coarsely, and boil in lightly salted water until tender (about 30 minutes). Do not let them become mushy.

Make the SHRIMP STUFFING: Chop the shrimp into ½-inch (1-cm) pieces. Combine the saké, *mirin*, and soy sauce in a saucepan, bring to a boil over high heat, add the shrimp, and cook over high heat, stirring constantly, until the shrimp turns pink. Drain.

When the potatoes are just tender, drain, return to a dry pan, and place over medium heat. Shake the pan to remove excess moisture from the potatoes. When they begin to lose their shape, remove from heat and immediately force through a fine drum sieve. Add the pinch salt, butter, two-thirds of the lightly beaten egg white, and 1½ Tbsps of the cornstarch. Mix well to form a firm "dough."

Divide the potato dough into 4 equal portions and form each into a round, slightly flat patty. Make a depression in the center of each patty, fill it with some of the shrimp stuffing, and work the potato up over the stuffing to form a smooth bun.

Prepare the SPINACH: Boil the spinach in lightly salted water until just tender, drain, and soak in cold water for 10 minutes. Combine the bonito stock, soy sauce, and *mirin* in a saucepan and bring to a boil over high heat. Cool. Drain the spinach, wring out excess water, and soak in the bonito stock seasoning.

Preheat a steamer over medium-high heat.

Dip the potato buns in the remaining egg white, then dust all over with the remaining cornstarch. Place in small heatproof serving bowls, then steam (in bowls) for 15 minutes. (Buns can also be steamed without bowls.)

Make the SILVER SAUCE: Combine the bonito stock, soy sauce, *mirin*, and salt in a saucepan. Bring to a boil over high heat and thicken with the cornstarch dissolved in water. Return to a boil, add the ginger juice, and immediately remove from heat.

Warm the spinach in its soaking liquid, drain, wring out some of the liquid, and cut into 1½-inch (4-cm) lengths.

Place in the serving bowls next to the potato buns, add some of the Silver Sauce, top with grated ginger, and serve.

250 Cals

Force potato through sieve

Stuff buns and close dough over filling

Grilled Eggplant

Yaki-nasu

Here is an easy way to prepare eggplant, that summer vegetable par excellence. Grilled quickly, skin and all, over a high flame, eggplants render some of their moisture but retain more of their flavor than with stewing or steaming, making this a popular dish in Japan both at home and in restaurants. Condiments might include not only dried bonito shavings, but also slivered scallions, ginger, or toasted sesame seeds.

Serves 4

4 Japanese eggplants, 5–6 oz (150 g) each, or 1¼ lbs (550 g) Western eggplant (see Note)

12 pods okra

¼ cup loose bonito threads or flakes (⅙ oz/ 5 g)

SEASONING

1⅔ cups (400 ml) bonito stock (*dashi*) (page 140)

2 Tbsps light soy sauce

1 tsp *mirin*

⅓ tsp salt

SOY-GINGER SAUCE

½ cup (120 ml) bonito stock (*dashi*) (page 140)

3 Tbsps dark soy sauce

2 tsps *mirin*

1 Tbsp fresh ginger juice (page 145)

Combine all the SEASONING ingredients in a saucepan, bring to a boil over high heat, and let cool.

Combine all the SOY-GINGER SAUCE ingredients, except the ginger juice, in a saucepan and bring to a boil over high heat. Let cool and then stir in the ginger juice.

Grill the eggplants on a wire net (or barbecue rack) over high heat. Test by pressing them with your finger: when the thickest part feels soft, they are done.

Plunge the eggplant in ice water to cool the exterior. Peel quickly, pat dry, and place in the seasoning liquid.

Trim the okra caps and dredge the pods in salt. Rub with a scouring motion to remove the tiny hairs.

Boil the okra in lightly salted water until just tender (about 2 minutes), plunge in cold water, drain, and pat dry. Cut in half lengthwise and carefully scrape out the seeds. Chop finely.

Drain the eggplant and cut into bite-sized pieces. Arrange in serving dishes and add a mound of the chopped okra. Spoon on a few tablespoons of the sauce and garnish with bonito threads (or flakes) before serving. Serve at room temperature or chilled.

55 cals

Grill eggplant and immediately plunge into ice water

Peel eggplant as soon as it is cool enough to handle

NOTE: For Western eggplant, slice into 1-inch (2½-cm) rounds, remove the skin, and make a shallow incision across the center of each round. Brush slices with oil and fry in a nonstick pan until tender (or cook peeled slices in a microwave oven until tender), then soak in seasoning liquid.

Deep-Fried Eggplant with Miso Sauce

Nasu dengaku

Foods of all sorts can be topped with hot seasoned miso—tofu, bamboo shoots, fish and shellfish, or eggplant as here. Miso toppings present a variety of possibilities; they can be made with either a white or red miso base and blended with a wide range of seasonings such as ground sansho pepper, grated ginger, toasted sesame seeds, hot yellow mustard (karashi), or red pepper.

Serves 4

vegetable oil for deep-frying
1 medium eggplant, about 10 oz (300 g)
1 Tbsp white poppy seeds, toasted in same way as sesame seeds (page 140)

RED MISO SAUCE

⅔ cup (150 g) red miso paste
1 egg yolk
7 Tbsps saké
6 Tbsps sugar
2½ Tbsps bonito stock (*dashi*) (page 140)

Combine all the RED MISO SAUCE ingredients in a double boiler and heat and stir until the paste almost reaches the same consistency as the miso before thinning (about 10 minutes).

Preheat the vegetable oil to a medium-low deep-frying temperature (330°–340° F/ 165°–170° C).

Cut the stems off the eggplant. Slice into ¾-inch (2-cm) rounds. Peel and pierce each round with a fork in several places.

Deep-fry the eggplant until tender (not crisp).

Top the slices of eggplant with sauce, sprinkle with poppy seed, and serve.

202 Cals

Deep-Fried Eggplant Sandwiches

Nasu hasami-age

People the world over seem to enjoy deep-fried eggplant—a natural if there ever was one. This recipe neatly sandwiches a chicken and a shrimp stuffing between slices of eggplant, the sandwich then deep-fried at a reduced temperature. Boiled potatoes, acorn squash, pumpkin, steamed sweet potatoes, raw zucchini, or even shiitake mushrooms can be substituted for the eggplant, while other fillings might include sliced scallops, ham, or cheese.

Serves 4

vegetable oil for deep-frying
½ medium eggplant (cut crosswise), about 5 oz (150 g)
flour

SHRIMP STUFFING

5 oz (150 g) shelled and deveined raw shrimp (page 48)
½ lightly beaten egg
1 Tbsp cornstarch dissolved in 1 Tbsp water
½ tsp salt

CHICKEN STUFFING

5 oz (150 g) ground chicken
½ lightly beaten egg
1 Tbsp cornstarch dissolved in 1 Tbsp water
1 Tbsp light soy sauce
1 tsp fresh ginger juice (page 145)

DIPPING SAUCE

1 cup (240 ml) bonito stock (*dashi*) (page 140)
¼ cup (60 ml) dark soy sauce
¼ cup (60 ml) *mirin*
¼ cup loose bonito flakes (⅙ oz/5 g)

CONDIMENTS

6 Tbsps finely grated daikon or white radish
4 Tbsps finely chopped and rinsed scallion
2 Tbsps finely grated fresh ginger

Make the SHRIMP STUFFING: Place the shrimp in a food processor, whir well, add remaining ingredients, and whir to a fine paste (or chop shrimp coarsely, grind in a mortar and pestle, then add ingredients in order and one at a time, grinding well as you go).

Make the CHICKEN STUFFING: Whir the chicken in a food processor, add the remaining ingredients, and whir to a smooth paste (or grind chicken in a mortar and pestle, then add remaining ingredients in order and one at a time, grinding with the addition of each new ingredient).

Make the DIPPING SAUCE: Combine the bonito stock, soy sauce, and *mirin* in a saucepan, bring to a boil over high heat, and add the dried bonito flakes. Immediately remove from heat and strain to clarify (page 142).

Preheat the vegetable oil to a medium-low deep-frying temperature (330°–340° F/165°–170° C).

Peel the eggplant, then cut into 4 wedges. Cut the wedges crosswise into ¼-inch (¾-cm) thick slices.

Pat the eggplant slices dry and dredge in flour. Spread some stuffing on a slice and top with another slice. Repeat, making as many sandwiches as possible.

Deep-fry the eggplant sandwiches for 3 minutes.

Arrange the sandwiches on serving plates, mound condiments alongside, and serve with lukewarm dipping sauce.

372 Cals

Spread on one stuffing and top with another slice

Vegetable-and-Shrimp Clusters

Satsuma-imo kaki-age

A mix of thinly sliced ingredients in tempura batter makes a quick side dish without all the time and trouble required to map out a full tempura dinner (page 130). In home cooking, shrimp or shellfish are often complemented with vegetables for frying in this way. Don't be discouraged if your clusters tend to lump together. Practice, the right consistency of batter, and the right frying temperature will yield a crisp, golden-brown filigree. These can be eaten as is, or served on top of rice or noodles for a light lunch.

Serves 4

1 large sweet potato, about 10 oz (300 g)

½ medium onion

2 fresh shiitake mushrooms, washed and stems removed, or 2 fresh brown mushrooms, washed and trimmed

2 stalks green asparagus, trimmed

vegetable oil for deep-frying

10 oz (300 g) small shrimp, shelled and deveined (page 48), or 5 oz (150 g) shucked scallops

flour

4 Tbsps finely grated daikon radish or white radish

DIPPING SAUCE

1 cup (240 ml) bonito stock (*dashi*) (page 140)

¼ cup (60 ml) dark soy sauce

¼ cup (60 ml) *mirin*

¼ cup loose bonito flakes (⅙ oz/5 g)

BATTER

1 large egg yolk

1 cup (240 ml) ice water

1 cup (120 g) sifted flour

Peel the potato and cut into very fine strips (⅛ × ⅛ × 2 inches [¼ × ¼ × 5 cm]). Soak in cold water for 10 minutes.

Slice the onion and mushrooms thinly. Cut the asparagus into strips the same size as the potato.

Make the DIPPING SAUCE: Combine the bonito stock, soy sauce, and *mirin* in a saucepan and bring to a boil over high heat. Add the bonito flakes, immediately remove from heat, and strain to clarify (page 142).

Preheat the oil to a medium deep-frying temperature (340° F/170° C).

Drain the sweet potato and pat dry. Combine the potato with the onion, mushroom, asparagus, and shrimp (or thinly sliced scallops) and mix well.

Sprinkle the mixture with flour and toss to coat lightly.

Make the BATTER: Combine the egg yolk and ice water in a bowl and add the flour all at once. Stir gently and briefly—the batter should be loose, runny, and half mixed, not sticky and well mixed.

Add the batter to the vegetables and mix gently to coat. Use a large spoon to drop loose clusters of the vegetable mixture into the hot oil. Fry 2 or 3 clusters at a time until golden brown.

Line serving plates with absorbent paper and arrange the clusters. Serve with bowls of lukewarm sauce flavored with small mounds of grated radish.

551 Cals

Slide clusters from spoon to oil

Turnip with Ginger-Miso Sauce

Furo-fuki kabura

Turnips and daikon radishes are wintertime favorites in Japan. Here turnips (carved in a straightforward symmetrical pattern with V-shaped notches) are simmered in a light kelp broth, then topped with Ginger-Miso Sauce—simplicity itself! The taste of the turnips comes straight through, so it is important to select only the most moist, tender, and fine-textured turnips. Acorn squash and leeks can be simmered in this way too, while eggplants, pumpkins, zucchini, or even figs or persimmons can be peeled, steamed, and topped with Ginger-Miso Sauce.

Serves 4

4 turnips, about ½ lb (220 g) each
4-inch (10-cm) length kelp (*konbu*)

GINGER-MISO SAUCE

1 cup (250 g) Red Miso Sauce (page 85)
¾ cup (150 ml) saké, alcohol burned off (page 147)
2½ Tbsps fresh ginger juice (page 145)

Cut off the tops and trim the bottoms of the turnips. Peel away all the tough outer skin, being careful to preserve the shape. Select 4 turnip leaves (for garnish) and parboil in lightly salted water, refresh in cold water, and drain.

Place the turnips, kelp, and 2 qts (2 L) water in a large saucepan, cover with a drop-lid (page 143), and bring to a boil over high heat. Reduce heat to low and simmer for about 30 minutes or until tender.

While the turnips are cooking, make the GINGER-MISO SAUCE: Place the Red Miso Sauce in a separate saucepan, thin with the saké, and bring to a boil over high heat. Add the ginger juice and stir.

When the turnips are done, drain well. Spoon several tablespoons of the sauce into each serving bowl, then place turnips on the bed of sauce. Pass the turnip leaves under hot tap water to reheat, then garnish the turnip.

90 Cals

Steamed Grated Turnip

Kabura-mushi

In Japan, turnips are used in many a winter dish. Here, moist sweet turnips are grated, mixed with rich grilled eel and vegetables, then steamed. Topped while still piping hot with the hot, clear sauce, there's nothing like it on a cold winter's day.

Serves 4

1 grilled eel (5 oz/150 g) (page 145)

4 raw shrimp, 1 oz (25 g) each, shelled and deveined (page 48)

2 oz (60 g) *shimeji*, oyster, or white mushrooms

1 oz (30 g) snow peas (about 10)

8 ginkgo nuts

2 turnips, 10 oz (300 g) each

1 egg white, lightly beaten

wasabi horseradish

SAUCE

1¼ cups (300 ml) bonito stock (*dashi*) (page 140)

1 Tbsp light soy sauce

1 Tbsp *mirin*

pinch salt

3 Tbsps cornstarch dissolved in 3 Tbsps water

Cut the grilled eel into ½ × 1½-inch (1 × 3-cm) strips.

Blanch the shrimp in boiling water until they turn pink, then immediately transfer to cold water. Cool, drain, pat dry, and cut into ½-inch (1½-cm) pieces.

Cut away the root end of the *shimeji* or oyster mushroom clusters and separate into small groups (or trim other mushrooms). Parboil in lightly salted water, refresh in cold water, and drain well.

String the snow peas, then sliver into ¾-inch (2-cm) long strips. Parboil in lightly salted water. Refresh in cold water, then drain.

Shell the ginkgo nuts and boil (page 141). Cut in half lengthwise.

Preheat a steamer over high heat.

Peel the turnips. Coarsely grate, then gently squeeze out some of the moisture with your fingers. Mix the turnip with the egg white and a pinch salt.

Combine the eel, shrimp, mushroom, ginkgo nuts, snow peas, and turnip. Mix well, then divide among four heatproof serving bowls.

Place the bowls in the preheated steamer and steam for 12–15 minutes.

Combine all the SAUCE ingredients, except the cornstarch, in a saucepan and bring to a boil over high heat. Thicken with the cornstarch dissolved in water. Return to a boil, then remove from heat.

Remove the bowls from the steamer, place on saucers, add some sauce to each, top with *wasabi* horseradish, and serve. Mix well before eating.

228 Cals

Chinese Cabbage and Deep-Fried Tofu

Hakusai usuage uma-ni

A favorite in many Japanese homes, this mildly flavored dish combines toothsome Chinese cabbage with slices of deep-fried tofu. Chinese cabbage leaves thicken considerably toward the bottom, so the thicker stalk is cut into thinner strips for easier cooking. Different kinds of tofu can also be used—thick deep-fried tofu (atsuage) or, for the very best taste, fresh, well-drained tofu deep-fried at home (see page 75). Served hot or cold, this is a remarkably useful dish, since it can be prepared well ahead of time or at short notice.

Serves 4

10 large leaves Chinese cabbage

1½-inch (4-cm) piece fresh ginger (⅔ oz/ 20 g)

4 pieces thin deep-fried tofu (*usuage*), about 3 oz (80 g) total

2 cups (480 ml) bonito stock (*dashi*) (page 140)

3 Tbsps *mirin*

5 tsps light soy sauce

1 Tbsp sugar

pinch salt

Cut the pale green leafy section from the thick stalk of each cabbage leaf. Cut the stalks into ½ × 2-inch (1½ × 5-cm) strips. Cut the leafy portions into 1 × 2-inch (3 × 5-cm) strips.

Cut the ginger with the grain into very fine slivers. Soak in cold water for 2–3 minutes, then drain.

Blanch the tofu in boiling water to remove any excess oil. Drain well in a colander and cut into ½ × 2-inch (1½ × 5-cm) strips.

Combine the remaining ingredients in a saucepan, then add the stalk strips, ginger slivers, and tofu. Cover with a drop-lid (page 143) and bring to a boil over high heat. Reduce heat to medium, simmer for 5 minutes, add the remaining cabbage, and heat through (about 3 minutes).

Arrange the Chinese cabbage and tofu in bowls, add several tablespoons of the pot liquid, and serve.

198 Cals

90

Roll to just cover filling

Fold in sides, finish rolling, and secure

Stuffed Cabbage, Japanese Style

Hakusai roru-ni

Cabbage rolls? Yes, but with a Japanese touch—saké, soy sauce, ginger, bonito stock, and mirin—flavors that can best soak in by leaving the rolls in the liquid after simmering. When eating with chopsticks, you should cut the rolls into manageable pieces before serving. Variations on the basic recipe might include lettuce or Western cabbage for Chinese cabbage, and ground shrimp, pork, or crab for the chicken.

Serves 4

4 large leaves Chinese cabbage
2 oz (60 g) snow peas (about 20)

STUFFING

7 oz (200 g) ground chicken
1 egg, lightly beaten
1 Tbsp saké
1 Tbsp dark soy sauce
½ tsp sugar
2 Tbsps cornstarch dissolved in 2 Tbsps water
dash fresh ginger juice (page 145)

SIMMERING

2½ cups (600 ml) bonito stock (*dashi*) (page 140)
3½ Tbsps light soy sauce
3½ Tbsps *mirin*

Make the STUFFING: Whir the chicken in a food processor, add the remaining ingredients, and whir well (or grind the chicken in a mortar and pestle, then add remaining stuffing ingredients in order and one at a time, grinding as you go).

Parboil the Chinese cabbage leaves until almost tender but still slightly firm, then drain, sprinkle lightly with salt, and cool. Pare away the thicker sections of the vein (page 126).

Place a portion of the stuffing at the base of a leaf, roll to just cover, fold in the edges, and roll up. Tie with kitchen string or secure with a toothpick.

Combine the SIMMERING ingredients in a saucepan and arrange the cabbage rolls in the bottom. Cover with a drop-lid (page 143) and bring to a boil over high heat. Reduce heat to low, simmer for 7–8 minutes, remove from heat, and allow the rolls to cool in the liquid to absorb the flavor.

String the snow peas, cut lengthwise into fine strips, and parboil in lightly salted water. Drain, refresh in cold water, and drain again.

When you are ready to serve, reheat the cabbage rolls in the simmering sauce, then add the snow peas and heat through. Remove the rolls, untie, cut into thirds, and arrange in bowls. Add the julienned snow peas and top with sauce.

192 Cals

Simmered Bamboo Shoot with *Wakame* Seaweed

Wakatake-ni

The Japanese treasure the tender young bamboo shoots that are brought to market in spring—as well they should, for the shoots can only be had fresh during a few brief weeks in March and April. Around the same time, a new harvest of fresh, not dried, wakame seaweed becomes available. Fresh or otherwise, these two treats of the season are often combined for an interesting contrast of textures firm and soft.

Serves 4

⅔ oz (20 g) dried *wakame* seaweed
¾ lb (340 g) canned whole bamboo shoots
1 cup loose bonito flakes (⅔ oz/20 g)
fresh dill

Place bonito flakes on gauze

Fold gauze over flakes

The finished "package"

SIMMERING

3⅓ cups (800 ml) bonito stock (*dashi*) (page 140)
7 Tbsps saké
3½ Tbsps *mirin*
3 Tbsps light soy sauce
1 Tbsp sugar
½ tsp salt

TO PREPARE

Soften and prepare the *wakame* seaweed (page 143). Cut into ¾-inch (2-cm) lengths.

Trim some of the tougher husk portions from the bottom of the bamboo shoots. Slice the thicker end of each shoot into ½-inch (1½-cm) thick rounds. Cut the remaining thin portion in quarters lengthwise. Wash well to scrub away any white residue. Bring the bamboo shoot to a boil over high heat in an ample amount of water, reduce heat to medium, and boil for 5 minutes.

Drain, then soak in cold water for 1 hour. Drain.

TO MAKE

Wrap the bonito flakes in gauze (and secure with kitchen string, if desired).

Combine all the SIMMERING ingredients in a saucepan, add the bamboo shoot and wrapped bonito flakes, and cover with a drop-lid (page 143). Bring to a boil over high heat, reduce heat to low, and simmer for 15 minutes. Remove from heat and let the bamboo shoot cool in the simmering liquid to absorb the flavor.

Reheat the bamboo shoot in the pot liquid, add the *wakame* seaweed, and simmer for 5 minutes. Serve with some simmering liquid. Garnish with dill.

53 Cals

Deep-Fried and Simmered Acorn Squash

Eikon sukasshu no age-ni

Combining the techniques of deep-frying and simmering does wonders for starchy vegetables (such as acorn squash, pumpkin, and potatoes), which tend to respond better to this pairing than to simmering alone. Deep-frying removes the excess moisture for a firmer texture, while bringing out a heartier flavor; simmering then seasons, leaving a full-bodied taste. Acorn squash is an especially sweet vegetable and browns very easily, so be sure to lower the temperature slightly for frying. Otherwise, try pan-frying thin slices of acorn squash in a small amount of oil before simmering.

Serves 4

vegetable oil for deep-frying

1 lb (450 g) acorn squash

2 blocks thick deep-fried tofu (*atsuage*), about 5 oz (150 g) total

1⅔ cups (400 ml) bonito stock (*dashi*) (page 140)

3½ Tbsps *mirin*

1 Tbsp sugar

4 Tbsps light soy sauce

2-inch (5-cm) piece fresh ginger, slivered (1 oz/30 g)

Preheat the oil to a low deep-frying temperature (300° F/150° C).

Cut the acorn squash into 8 equal sections, then peel. Round the edges of each piece.

Cut each piece of tofu into 4 triangles. Boil for 3 minutes and drain to remove any excess oil.

Deep-fry the acorn squash until the outer surface browns slightly. (This may also be done in a frying pan—simply fry the thin slices of squash in a little oil over high heat until they brown.)

Place the bonito stock in a saucepan, add the acorn squash and tofu, cover with a drop-lid (page 143), and bring to a boil over high heat. Reduce the heat to low and simmer for 2-3 minutes. Add the *mirin* and sugar and simmer for another 5 minutes. Add the soy sauce and simmer for a final 10 minutes.

While the squash is simmering, cut the ginger with the grain into very fine slivers. Soak in cold water for 2-3 minutes, then drain.

Transfer the squash to bowls and top with slivered ginger before serving.

279 Cals

Simmered Soybeans

Nimame

This traditional Japanese favorite takes soy-beans—now very much in the public eye as a major protein food—and cooks them slowly for full flavor. Here konbu kelp has been added to enhance the taste of the soybeans, but chicken, pork, or beef might also be added for a stronger accent. The real secret to this recipe, however, is to allow the beans a long pre-soak before even beginning to cook.

Serves 4

1 cup (120 g) dried soybeans
4-inch (10-cm) length kelp (*konbu*)
2½ cups (600 ml) bonito stock (*dashi*) (page 140)
2 Tbsps sugar
5 tsps *mirin*
3 Tbsps light soy sauce
fresh rosemary

TO PREPARE

Soak the soybeans overnight in about 5 times their volume of cold water.

TO MAKE

Drain the soybeans, place in a large saucepan with ample water, cover with a drop-lid (page 143), and bring to a boil over high heat. Reduce heat to low and boil for 10 minutes. Drain, plunge into cold water, and drain again.

Cut the kelp into ¼-inch (½-cm) squares. Combine the soybeans, kelp, and bonito stock in a soup pot, cover with a drop-lid, and bring to a boil over high heat. Reduce heat to low and boil for 10 minutes.

Add the sugar and *mirin* and simmer for 5 minutes. Add the soy sauce and simmer for 5 minutes without disturbing the beans, then continue simmering until the liquid is almost gone, shaking the pot occasionally to coat all the beans evenly.

Garnish with rosemary. Serve hot or at room temperature.

191 Cals

Deep-Fried Zucchini

Zukkini iri-dashi

Eggplants and tofu are more typically dredged in cornstarch and deep-fried in this manner, but zucchini—still a novelty in Japan—proves a natural here. Cut into fairly thick rounds, the zucchini will remain moist inside while the light coating of starch on the surface fries

Sautéed Celery with Sesame

Serori kinpira

Sliced vegetables sautéed until tender, then seasoned with splashes of saké and soy sauce and a pinch of salt are simple and delicious. In Japan, burdock root is unquestionably the most likely candidate for this treatment to a crackling crispiness. Acorn squash or other similar fleshy vegetables can be substituted for zucchini.

Serves 4

vegetable oil for deep-frying
4 zucchini, about ½ lb (220 g) each
cornstarch

SAUCE

1 cup (240 ml) bonito stock (*dashi*) (page 140)
4½ Tbsps dark soy sauce
4½ Tbsps *mirin*
¼ cup loose bonito flakes (⅙ oz/5 g)

CONDIMENTS

1 Tbsp finely grated fresh ginger
2 Tbsps finely chopped and rinsed scallion

Preheat the oil to a medium deep-frying temperature (340° F/170° C).

Peel the zucchini and wash. Drain, pat dry, and cut into ¼-inch (½-cm) rounds. Coat well in cornstarch.

Deep-fry the zucchini until the surface becomes crispy (about 2 minutes).

Make the SAUCE: Combine the bonito stock, soy sauce, and *mirin* and bring to a boil over high heat. Add the bonito flakes, then remove from heat and strain to clarify (page 142).

Arrange the zucchini in bowls, spoon in several tablespoons of the sauce, and add grated ginger and chopped scallion.

172 Cals

(called kinpira), *but any crunchy vegetable such as lotus root, carrot, or celery root, or even acorn squash, sweet potato, or potato, not to mention* konnyaku, *are excellent prepared in this way. Eaten hot as a side dish, or cold as a salad on picnics, this is sure to become a favorite.*

Serves 4

2 Tbsps white sesame seeds, toasted (page 140)
3 stalks celery
1 Tbsp vegetable oil
2 tsps saké
pinch sugar
4 tsps dark soy sauce
ground red pepper

Place the sesame seeds on a dry cloth and chop coarsely with a knife.

String the celery and cut into ¼ × ¼ × 2-inch (½ × ½ × 5-cm) strips.

Heat the oil in a frying pan over high heat and sauté the celery. When it becomes tender (about 1 minute), add the saké and sugar. Simmer until the liquid is almost gone, then add the soy sauce. Continue simmering until most of the liquid boils away, then season with red pepper to taste.

Transfer to bowls, top with the sesame seed, and serve.

71 Cals

Vegetables with White Sesame Dressing

Goshiki yasai gomashirasu-ae

White Sesame Dressing made with blended tofu is a Japanese classic, although here it is used on a Western-style salad with quite pleasing results. Aside from very spicy or pungent ones, almost any vegetable can be used. They should be selected for their appearance as well as taste.

Serves 4

1 head Belgian endive, about 5 oz (150 g)
4 red radishes
2 shallots
4 stalks green asparagus, trimmed
½ head broccoli

WHITE SESAME DRESSING

1 block regular ("cotton") tofu, about 10 oz (300 g)
3 Tbsps sesame paste (page 140)
3 Tbsps sugar
1 tsp salt
1 tsp light soy sauce
3 Tbsps rice vinegar
2 tsps *mirin*, alcohol burned off (page 146)
2 Tbsps bonito stock (*dashi*) (page 140)

TO PREPARE

Press out moisture from tofu for 1 hour (page 74).

TO MAKE

Combine all the WHITE SESAME DRESSING ingredients in a food processor and whir to a smooth paste (or force well-drained tofu through a fine drum sieve, grind in a mortar and pestle, and then add remaining ingredients in order and one at a time, grinding well as you go). Force through a sieve.

Cut the endive and radish into fine julienne strips. Soak the radish in cold water.

Slice the shallots thinly and soak in water.

Boil the asparagus and broccoli separately in lightly salted water until just tender, refresh in ice water, and drain. Cut the asparagus into fine julienne strips and break the broccoli into small florets.

Drain all the vegetables well, make a mound of each on the serving dish around a mound of dressing. Serve.

90 Cals

Marinated Watercress

Kuresson hitashi

One of the more popular culinary techniques employed in the Japanese kitchen is that in which a vegetable is blanched and then doused in a light seasoning liquid to absorb just a hint of flavor. The vegetable most commonly prepared in this style is spinach, but watercress as here, endive, corn salad, and even alfalfa sprouts are also excellent. A stronger accent can be provided by adding lemon or ginger juice, toasted sesame seeds, or other flavor accents.

Serves 4

½ lb (220 g) watercress, trimmed
vegetable oil for deep-frying
1 Tbsp pine nuts

SEASONING

2 cups (480 ml) bonito stock (*dashi*) (page 140)
¼ cup (60 ml) light soy sauce
¼ cup (60 ml) *mirin*
pinch salt

Boil the watercress in lightly salted water until just tender, refresh in ice water, then drain and gently wring out excess moisture.

Combine the SEASONING ingredients in a saucepan, bring to a boil over high heat, then let cool.

Soak the watercress in the cooled seasoning mixture for 30 minutes or until ready to serve (whichever is longer).

Preheat the oil to a medium (340° F/ 170° C) temperature and deep-fry the pine nuts. Slice.

Remove the watercress from the seasoning, wring gently, and cut into 1½-inch (4-cm) lengths.

Arrange the watercress in bowls and pour an ample amount of the seasoning liquid into each bowl. Top with sliced pine nuts and serve.

44 Cals

Okra and Coddled Egg with *Wasabi* Sauce

Okura wasabi-joyu

Okra, though not native to Japan, has in recent years become a favorite with Japanese cooks. Here, it is boiled, scraped of the slightly bitter seeds, and briskly chopped to a syrupy pulp, its smooth texture complemented by that of the Coddled Egg. Tangy Soy-Ginger Sauce (page 84) or Three-Flavors Dressing (page 49) may be substituted for the Wasabi Sauce for equally delicious results.

Serves 4

4 eggs
25 pods okra

¼ cup loose bonito threads or flakes (⅙ oz/ 5 g)

WASABI SAUCE

¾ cup (180 ml) saké, alcohol burned off (page 147)
6 Tbsps dark soy sauce
2 Tbsps *mirin*
¼ cup loose bonito flakes (⅙ oz/5 g)
1 Tbsp fresh grated (or 2 tsps reconstituted) *wasabi* horseradish

TO PREPARE

Make the WASABI SAUCE: Combine the saké, soy sauce, and *mirin* in a saucepan and bring to a boil over high heat. Remove from heat, add the bonito flakes, and cool quickly by placing the pan in a bowl of ice water. Strain to clarify (page 142).

TO MAKE

Make the Coddled Eggs (page 69).

Trim the okra caps, then dredge the pods in salt and rub with a scouring motion to remove the small hairs from the skin of the pods.

Drop the pods in lightly salted boiling water and cook until just tender. Refresh in cold water, drain, and pat dry. Cut in half lengthwise and scrape out the seeds.

Chop the okra crosswise into thin slices and then continue chopping until it becomes sticky.

Add the *wasabi* horseradish to the sauce.

Crack 1 egg open and let it gently fall into a bowl of cold water. Scoop it up in the palm of your hand, and while the egg is still submerged roll it back and forth gently in your palm and separate the egg white from the yolk. Discard the egg white and place the yolk in the serving bowl on top of the okra. Repeat with remaining eggs.

Spoon in some sauce, top with bonito threads (or flakes), and serve.

130 Cals

Spinach with Sesame Dressing

Horenso goma-ae

Tender spinach tossed in an aromatic Sesame Dressing makes an appetizing addition to any meal. The secret is in using fresh sesame seeds and carefully blending or grinding them to a coarse paste. Broccoli, corn salad, endive, and other leafy green vegetables also go deliciously with Sesame Dressing, and by substituting cashew or macadamia nuts for the sesame seeds there are even more possibilities for this recipe.

Serves 4

1 lb (450 g) spinach

SEASONING

1⅔ cups (400 ml) bonito stock (*dashi*) (page 140)
2 Tbsps dark soy sauce

SESAME DRESSING

⅔ cup (90 g) white sesame seeds, toasted (page 140)
4 tsps sugar
2½ Tbsps dark soy sauce
7 Tbsps bonito stock (*dashi*) (page 140)

Score the root of the untrimmed spinach bunch in a cross (if it has not been trimmed off by the greengrocer). Cook in lightly salted boiling water until just tender, then soak in ice water for 10 minutes.

Drain the spinach and wring out as much excess water as possible. Cut off any tough stem ends and discard. Cut the spinach into 1-inch (3-cm) lengths.

Soak the spinach in the SEASONING ingredients.

Combine all the SESAME DRESSING ingredients in a blender and mix well (or grind the sesame seeds in a mortar and pestle, then add the ingredients in order and one at a time, grinding well as you go).

Drain the spinach and gently wring out the excess liquid. Combine it with the dressing and toss well. Use a wooden spoon to gently pound the spinach. Serve.

183 Cals

Rice

Rice Balls

Onigiri

Rice Balls made of white rice, salt, and bits of other ingredients make a convenient finger food. An added bonus is that they are just as good cold as they are hot so they are perfect for lunch boxes and take-along snacks. With different stuffings and toppings, almost endless variations are possible. But whatever flavor combinations you choose, remember the individual grains of rice should hold together without being crushed; the trick is to shape and press just enough to hold the ball together.

Makes 20 balls

4 cups (680 g) uncooked short-grain rice plus 5¾ cups (1380 ml) water

1½ tsps salt

1 sheet *nori* seaweed

Japanese pickles (optional)

FOR FILLINGS

½ lb (220 g) salmon fillet

2 large pickled plums (*umeboshi*)

3 oz (90 g) salted kelp (*shio konbu*) (page 146)

¼ cup loose bonito flakes (⅙ oz/5 g)

1½ tsps dark soy sauce

TOPPINGS

1 Tbsp white sesame seeds

1 Tbsp black sesame seeds

TO PREPARE

Sprinkle the salmon fillet with salt and let stand for 2 hours.

Wash the rice thoroughly (page 101) and let stand for 30–60 minutes.

TO MAKE

Cook the rice (page 101).

While rice is cooking, prepare FILLINGS and TOPPINGS.

Remove the pits from the pickled plums. Chop the plums coarsely.

Cut the salted kelp into thin strips.

Mix together the dried bonito flakes and soy sauce.

Toast the black and white sesame seeds (page 140).

Wash the salt off of the salmon fillet, pat dry, and grill on a wire net over a hot flame for 3–5 minutes (or use an oven broiler). Use a fork to break the fish into small pieces.

When the rice has finished cooking, add the salt and mix well.

TO SHAPE

Combine 2 cups of unpacked cooked rice with the salmon and mix gently but thoroughly. Wet your hands with salted water (1½ tsps salt to 1 cup [240 ml] water) and take one-fourth of the rice-salmon mixture and form into a cylinder or triangle. Make 3 more balls. Re-wet your hands as necessary.

Wet your hands with salted water. Take ½ cup unpacked cooked rice and form into a loose ball. Force one-fourth of the pickled plum (or other filling) into the center and close the rice over it. Form into a triangle or cylinder. Make 4 balls of each filling (pickled plum, salted kelp, and bonito flakes soaked in soy sauce).

Make 4 plain triangles or cylinders.

Triangle: Take a roughly formed ball of rice (with filling added) in your cupped left hand, and with the bent fingers of your right hand begin shaping. Rotate rice to shape by gently tossing between cupped hands, and continue shaping sides and edges as you go. Mold the rice firmly but gently, pressing just hard enough to hold rice together. Do not mash.

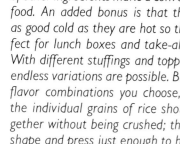

Cylinder: Take a roughly formed ball of rice (with filling added) in your left hand, close fingers over rice, and crimp. Rotate and crimp again to finish the basic shape, then smooth ends and sides with the fingers of your right hand as necessary. Again, press gently and do not mash the rice.

Toast the *nori* seaweed over a high gas flame if it has not been pretoasted (page 143). Cut crosswise into 1- to 2-inch (3- to 4-cm) wide strips.

Sprinkle sesame seeds over some of the rice shapes or wrap with *nori* seaweed, then garnish with Japanese pickles and serve.

151 Cals

Place filling in center

Shape rice into triangle

Mixed Rice

Kayaku gohan

Cutting the vegetables finely and achieving just the right balance of vegetables and other ingredients to rice are the keys to good Mixed Rice. This is not only a matter of taste and appearance; the amount of water and the cooking time will vary in proportion to how much moisture is in the particular vegetables. The rice in the bottom of the pan may scorch a little from the soy sauce, but all the better for giving the rest of the rice a pleasant, toasted scent. Chicken, thin deep-fried tofu, duck, shellfish, and white-fleshed fish are among the many possibilities for Mixed Rice.

Serves 4

2½ cups (425 g) uncooked short-grain rice

4 oz (120 g) boned chicken thigh

½ small carrot

4 fresh shiitake mushrooms, washed and stems removed, or 4 fresh brown mushrooms, washed and trimmed

⅓ cake *konnyaku*, about 3 oz (90 g)

2 oz (60 g) snow peas (about 20)

3 Tbsps saké

1 sheet *nori* seaweed

FOR COOKING RICE

3 cups (720 ml) bonito stock (*dashi*) (page 140)

4 Tbsps dark soy sauce

3 Tbsps *mirin*

¾ tsp salt

Wash the rice and let stand for 30–60 minutes (page 101).

Dice the chicken into ¼-inch (½-cm) cubes, drop in boiling water for a moment until it turns white, cool in cold water, and drain.

Cut the carrot into fine julienne strips about 1 inch (3 cm) long. Thinly slice the mushrooms.

Cut the *konnyaku* into thin strips ¼ inch (½ cm) wide and 1 inch (3 cm) long. Sprinkle with salt and scrub, then boil (page 142). Drain and let cool.

String the snow peas and cut lengthwise into fine strips. Parboil in lightly salted water, refresh in cold water, and drain.

Combine the uncooked rice, bonito stock, soy sauce, *mirin*, and salt in a large, heavy-bottomed saucepan. Add the chicken, carrot, mushroom, and *konnyaku*. Mix well, cover, and then cook following the directions for cooking rice on page 101.

When the rice has finished boiling but before it is set aside to stand, sprinkle with the saké and snow peas. Place a piece of cheesecloth or a clean, dry kitchen towel over the pot and replace the lid, then let stand for 10–15 minutes.

Toast the *nori* seaweed over a high gas flame (if it has not been pretoasted), then crumble (page 143).

Mix the rice and other ingredients gently but thoroughly. Sprinkle with crumbled *nori* seaweed just before serving.

475 Cals

Chicken and Egg on Rice

Oyako donburi

For a quick lunch, try a typical Japanese meal-in-a-bowl. One of the most popular is Chicken and Egg on Rice, affectionately called Mother-and-Child Bowl in Japanese. Make sure you cook the egg topping only until it is half-cooked, or just set.

Serves 4

2½ cups (425 g) uncooked short-grain rice plus 3½ cups (840 ml) water
5 oz (150 g) boned chicken
½ medium onion
2 scallions
6 eggs, lightly beaten

SAUCE

1⅔ cups (400 ml) bonito stock (*dashi*) (page 140) or chicken stock
4½ Tbsps dark soy sauce
2½ Tbsps light soy sauce
2 Tbsps *mirin*
2 Tbsps sugar

Wash the rice and let stand for 30–60 minutes, then cook (page 101).

Cut the chicken into ½-inch (1-cm) cubes, drop in boiling water just until the color changes, then transfer to cold water and drain.

Slice the onion thinly. Cut the scallions diagonally into thin rounds.

Combine all the SAUCE ingredients in a saucepan and boil over high heat, stirring constantly, until the sugar is dissolved.

Make 1 serving at a time. Transfer one-fourth of the sauce to a small, clean saucepan,

add one-fourth of the chicken and onion, and place over high heat. When the chicken is

Pour in egg to cover as much surface area as possible

done, add the scallion, then pour in one-fourth of the lightly beaten egg in a broad, circular motion to cover as much surface area as possible. When the outer edges of the egg begin to set, stir through once in an X motion with chopsticks or a fork. Fill a deep soup bowl with 1 portion of the hot cooked rice, and when the egg is partially, or soft, set slide the chicken-egg-onion mixture in its sauce onto the rice. Cover.

Repeat, making the remaining 3 servings.

629 Cals

HOW TO COOK RICE

Washing: Place the rice in a bowl, add ample cold water, stir through once or twice, and immediately pour off cloudy water. Knead the rice with your palm but do not grind.

Add ample fresh water and stir vigorously. Discard the water. Repeat until water is no longer milky, stirring vigorously with each rinsing, but again, not so strongly that you grind the grains of rice.

Draining: Pour the rice into a colander and let stand for 30–60 minutes to allow the rice to expand.

Cooking: Add the rice and water to a heavy-bottomed saucepan, cover, and bring slowly to a boil over medium heat.

When the water boils, increase heat to high and boil for 3 minutes, then reduce heat to medium and boil 5 minutes. Do not let the pot boil over. Foam should issue from the pot, but adjust the heat as necessary if the pot continually boils over.

Reduce the heat to low and boil a final 5 minutes. Remove from heat, uncover and quickly place a piece of cheesecloth over the pot. Replace the lid and let stand for 10–15 minutes to finish cooking. Note that the rice is not done until after it has been allowed to stand.

Sushi

Decorative Sushi

Bijutsu-zushi

*Professional sushi chefs have a large reper-
toire of decorative sushi that they prepare for
special occasions. The three selections here—
all simple to prepare at home—allow the
home cook to mount his or her own impres-
sive display of sushi. Tazuna-maki resemble
the rope once used for horses' reins. Naruto-
maki are swirled like whirlpools, and so take
their name from the famous Naruto Whirlpools on Japan's Inland Sea. Temari-zushi
are shaped like the colorful brocade balls that
children play with.*

Wrap fish in kelp before refrigerating

Serves 4

kelp (*konbu*) reserved from making bonito stock (optional)
2½ cups (425 g) uncooked short-grain rice plus 3¼ cups (780 ml) water
sweet-vinegared ginger (*amazu-shoga*)

MARINADE

2 cups (480 ml) rice vinegar
⅔ cup (160 ml) water
2 Tbsps sugar
2-inch (5-cm) length kelp (*konbu*)

SUSHI DRESSING (see Note)

½ cup (120 ml) rice vinegar
5½ Tbsps sugar
1½ Tbsps salt
1-inch (2½-cm) length kelp (*konbu*)

FOR *TAZUNA-MAKI*

4 oz (120 g) flatfish fillet such as flounder, halibut, or turbot
4 raw shrimp, 1 oz (30 g) each
1½ oz (45 g) snow peas (about 20)
3 oz (90 g) smoked salmon fillet

HAND VINEGAR

1 cup (240 ml) water plus 2 Tbsps rice vinegar

FOR *TEMARI-ZUSHI*

4 oz (120 g) sea bream or white-fleshed fish fillet
1 hard-boiled egg
4 oz (120 g) smoked salmon fillet
wasabi horseradish
1 Tbsp black sesame seeds, toasted (page 140)

FOR *NARUTO-MAKI*

5 oz (150 g) squid, cleaned and skinned (page 141)
⅛ cucumber (cut lengthwise)
1 Tbsp white sesame seeds, toasted (page 140)
2 sheets *nori* seaweed, toasted (page 143)
4 oz (120 g) sea urchin

4 bamboo skewers
bamboo rolling mat (page 143)

TO PREPARE

Sprinkle the flatfish and sea bream with salt and let stand for 40 minutes.

Remove any small bones from salted fish with tweezers, then wash fish. Combine all the MARINADE ingredients and soak the fish until surface turns white (about 5 minutes), then drain in a colander for about 1 hour.

Wrap the fish in a piece of kelp left over from making bonito stock, than wrap in plastic wrap and refrigerate for 5 hours.

Combine the SUSHI DRESSING ingredients for the sushi rice in a saucepan over high heat. When the sugar has dissolved, set the saucepan in a bowl of ice water and force-cool the dressing.

Wash the rice well and let it drain for 30-60 minutes (page 101).

TO MAKE

Cook the rice (page 101).

When the rice has finished cooking, turn it out into a large wooden bowl. Slowly pour ⅔ cup (160 ml) or slightly less dressing over the hot rice and "slice" across the rice with a slashing, rather than a circular, motion, using a rice paddle or flat wooden spoon. Mix well and let cool to about body temperature. When cool, mound the rice in the center and cover the bowl with a damp cloth.

TO ASSEMBLE *TAZUNA-MAKI*

Skewer the shrimp from the underside beginning at the head. Boil for 3 minutes in lightly salted water, transfer to cold water to cool, and then remove the skewers. Shell and pinch off the heads and tails. Make an incision on the underside the length of the shrimp, cutting almost through to remove the vein. Open the shrimp, spread it flat, slice in half horizontally, then cut lengthwise into ¼-inch (¾-cm) wide strips. Trim the strips to 1½ inches (4 cm).

Cut the marinated flatfish into strips the same size as the shrimp.

String the snow peas and boil in lightly salted water until just tender. Refresh in cold water, drain well, and cut into very thin

TO PREPARE SUSHI RICE

Add Sushi Dressing to rice

Mix rice by cutting across it in a slashing motion, then let cool to body temperature

TAZUNA-MAKI

Place log of sushi rice on bamboo rolling mat

Grip mat and finish shaping log by raising and lowering mat ends

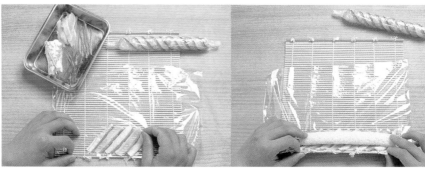

Lay out strips of ingredients on plastic wrap

Carefully lift up end closest to you and roll

TEMARI-ZUSHI

Parch egg yolk

Place small ball of rice on square of fish seasoned with *wasabi*

Close gauze over fish and rice, then twist to press and shape

Make a shallow depression on top

Fill depression with egg yolk or sesame

(¹⁄₁₆-inch/¹⁄₅-cm) strips the same length as the shrimp and flatfish.

Cut the salmon into thin strips of the same dimensions as the snow peas.

Moisten your hands with HAND VINEGAR. Form about ⅓ cup unpacked sushi rice into a loose log and roll in a bamboo rolling mat until it is about 1 inch (2 cm) in diameter. The rice will have to be worked, almost kneaded, into shape. Make 3 more logs.

Line the bamboo rolling mat with plastic wrap. Lay out the ingredients diagonally. Frame the wider bands of shrimp and flatfish with a thin strip of snow pea and salmon on each side (as shown): shrimp, salmon, snow pea, flatfish, salmon, snow pea. Repeat to the end of the mat.

Lay the roll on top of the strips and carefully roll up. Press and shape the roll, remove the bamboo mat, and set aside. Make 3 more rolls. Cut into 1½-inch (4-cm) lengths, then unwrap each piece.

TO ASSEMBLE *TEMARI-ZUSHI*

Force the yolk of the hard-boiled egg through a fine drum sieve, add a pinch salt, and parch in a dry frying pan over low heat until it becomes crumbly.

Slice the smoked salmon into 1½-inch (4-cm) square pieces about ⅛ inch (¼ cm) thick. Repeat with the sea bream.

Make 24 small, loose balls of sushi rice about 1 inch (3 cm) in diameter. Soak a piece of gauze in Hand Vinegar and wring it out well. Set a square of fish on the gauze, season

with a small amount of *wasabi* horseradish, and place a small ball of rice on the fish, then wrap the gauze around the sushi and twist to finish shaping. Make a shallow depression in the center of the top with your finger, unwrap, and sprinkle with either egg yolk (for salmon) or sesame seed (for sea bream). Finish the rest of the balls, re-wetting the gauze as necessary.

TO ASSEMBLE *NARUTO-MAKI*

Cut the squid into thin (¼-inch/½-cm) strips as long as possible.

Peel and seed the cucumber wedge and cut lengthwise into 4 narrow strips.

Mix the remaining sushi rice with the sesame seeds. Lay a sheet of the *nori* seaweed lengthwise on a bamboo rolling mat, shiny side down. Place half the remaining rice on the closer two-thirds of the *nori* sheet and spread it to the edges.

Lay out a strip of cucumber 1 inch (3 cm) from the edge closest to you, and then at ½-inch (1-cm) intervals a strip of squid, a row

of sea urchin, and final strips of squid and cucumber.

To roll, curl up the edge closest to you, press with mat, roll up 1 inch (3 cm) more, press, and continue to the end of the rice. Finish rolling, then correct the shape by pressing the mat. Make 1 more roll.

Cut each roll into 8 rounds about ¾ inch (1½ cm) wide.

TO SERVE

Arrange each type of sushi on its own serving platter or place several pieces of each sushi on individual plates. Garnish with well-drained sweet-vinegared ginger.

809 Cals

NOTE: Sushi Dressing will keep indefinitely under refrigeration if placed in a tightly sealed jar. It actually improves with age, and dressing that has been aged at least 2–3 weeks is best. For larger amounts, combine 1 qt (1 L) rice vinegar, 3 cups (600 g) sugar, ¾ cup (200 g) salt, and 4-inch (10-cm) length kelp (*konbu*). Let stand 24 hours, remove the kelp, and prepare in the same manner.

NARUTO-MAKI

Lay out ingredients at 1-inch (3-cm) intervals

Roll up

Side view showing swirled *nori* seaweed

Scattered Sushi

Bara-zushi

The simplest, most popular home-style variety of sushi is Scattered Sushi. Unlike Nigiri Sushi (page 110), no raw ingredients are used—everything is cooked, either simmered with soy sauce or marinated in vinegar before adding to the sushi rice—so Scattered Sushi can be made ahead or taken on outings

without fear of spoiling. Topped with thin slivered omelette, succulent simmered mushrooms, and pink shrimp, this makes an eye-catching and festive party dish.

Serves 4

8 dried shiitake mushrooms

2 oz (60 g) dried baby shrimp

8 ft (2.5 m) dried gourd ribbons (*kanpyo*) (1 oz/30 g)

1 cake freeze-dried tofu (*Koya-dofu*), about ½ oz (15 g)

2 oz (60 g) dried baby sardines (*shirasu-boshi*) (optional)

2½ cups (425 g) uncooked short-grain rice plus 3¼ cups (780 ml) water

8 raw shrimp, 1 oz (25 g) each

3–4 oz (90–120 g) snow peas (about 40)

4 sheets *nori* seaweed

SUSHI DRESSING (see Note, page 105)

1¼ cups (300 ml) rice vinegar

14 Tbsps sugar

3⅔ Tbsps salt

2-inch (5-cm) length kelp (*konbu*)

FOR SIMMERING MUSHROOMS AND GOURD RIBBONS

1¼ cups (300 ml) bonito stock (*dashi*) (page 140)

3½ Tbsps water from soaking shiitake mushrooms

2 Tbsps sugar

1 Tbsp *mirin*

2 Tbsps dark soy sauce

FOR SIMMERING TOFU

1⅔ cups (400 ml) bonito stock (*dashi*) (page 140)

3½ Tbsps sugar

3 Tbsps light soy sauce

⅓ tsp salt

THIN OMELETTES

3 eggs, lightly beaten

pinch salt

vegetable oil

4 bamboo skewers

TO PREPARE

Soak the mushrooms for 6–7 hours (page 142). Reserve water.

Scrub soaked gourd ribbons with salt

Make the SUSHI DRESSING (page 104).

Soak the dried shrimp in ½ cup (120 ml) Sushi Dressing for 4–5 hours.

Soak the gourd ribbons in water for 10 minutes, drain, then sprinkle with salt and scrub to remove the odor and firm up. Drop the salty gourd ribbons in boiling water and cook until tender (about 5 minutes). Spread on a rack to cool.

Simmer the gourd ribbons and softened mushrooms: Combine in a saucepan with the bonito stock and 3½ Tbsps water reserved from soaking mushrooms. Cover with a drop-lid (page 143) and bring to a boil over high heat. Reduce heat to low and simmer for 5 minutes. Add the sugar and *mirin* and simmer for 5 more minutes. Add the soy sauce and continue simmering until only a small amount of the liquid remains in the bottom. Drain, reserving liquid.

Reconstitute the tofu and then remove the cloudy liquid from it (page 81). Place in a saucepan with bonito stock, cover with a drop-lid, then bring to a boil over high heat, reduce the heat to low, and simmer for 5 minutes. Add the sugar and simmer for 5 more minutes. Add the soy sauce and salt and simmer for a final 5 minutes. Remove from heat and let soak in the liquid to absorb flavor.

Blanch the dried fish in boiling water, drain in colander and then soak for 1 hour in ½ cup (120 ml) Sushi Dressing.

Wash the rice well and let stand for 30–60 minutes (page 101).

TO MAKE

Cook the rice (page 101).

Devein the shrimp (page 48) and thread on bamboo skewers on the underside from head to tail. Boil in lightly salted water for about 3 minutes, then drop in cold water and let cool. Pat dry, remove the skewers, and shell, removing both the head and tail. Slice crosswise into ½-inch (1-cm) pieces.

String the snow peas, boil in lightly salted water until just tender, refresh in cold water, and drain. Leave half the snow peas whole (trim bottoms if desired) and cut the other half into fine julienne strips.

Make the THIN OMELETTES: Beat the eggs lightly, add the salt, and pour through a fine sieve. Heat a frying pan or a crepe pan over medium heat and use a paper-towel swab to oil the pan. Pour a small amount of the egg into the pan to test the temperature—it should cook gently and noiselessly; adjust the heat if necessary. Pour in enough of the egg to coat the bottom of the pan thinly. Fry just until the edges of the omelette set, then turn carefully. Fry the other side for only a moment, remove omelette from pan, pat between paper toweling to remove any excess oil, and let cool. Repeat with remaining egg. Cut into fine julienne strips.

Combine half of the mushrooms and gourd ribbon in a food processor and whir until finely shredded (or chop finely). Drain the tofu and cut into thin strips ¼ inch (½ cm) wide and ¾ inch (1½ cm) long.

Transfer the hot cooked rice to a large wooden bowl and gradually mix in ⅔ cup (160 ml) Sushi Dressing or slightly less to taste by slicing across the rice (page 104).

Drain the baby sardines and dried shrimp. When the rice has cooled to about body temperature, stir in the dried shrimp, dried fish, julienned snow peas, mushroom–gourd ribbon mixture, and freeze-dried tofu. Add 2 Tbsps liquid reserved from simmering mushrooms and mix thoroughly.

Toast the *nori* seaweed over a hot flame if it has not been pretoasted, then crumble (page 143).

Cut the remaining mushroom caps in half diagonally.

Transfer the rice to serving bowl, top first with *nori* seaweed and then with egg threads. Arrange the mushroom, shrimp, and whole snow peas on top of egg.

804 Cals

Oil pan with swab

Cook Thin Omelette until edges set

Turn and cook briefly on other side

Bo Sushi

Bo-zushi

Sushi topped with thick fillets of vinegared or grilled fish that are pressed into a block with a bamboo rolling mat is called Bo Sushi. The rice for Bo Sushi is worked to a slightly stickier consistency than for ordinary Nigiri Sushi. What's more, the flavor improves if the assembled sushi is allowed to sit for half a day or more.

Slice open sea bream

Peel away translucent layer from mackerel

Serves 8

14 oz (400 g) sea bream or white-fleshed fish fillet, with skin

kelp (*konbu*) reserved from making bonito stock (optional)

1¾–2 lbs (800 g) mackerel fillet, with skin

2½ cups (425 g) uncooked short-grain rice plus 3¼ cups (780 ml) water

sweet-vinegared ginger (*amazu-shoga*)

MARINADE

2 cups (480 ml) rice vinegar

⅔ cup (160 ml) water

2 Tbsps sugar

2-inch (5-cm) length kelp (*konbu*)

SUSHI DRESSING (see Note, page 105)

½ cup (120 ml) rice vinegar

5½ Tbsps sugar

1½ Tbsps salt

1-inch (2½-cm) length kelp (*konbu*)

HAND VINEGAR

1 cup (240 ml) water plus 2 Tbsps rice vinegar

bamboo rolling mat (page 143)

TO PREPARE

Sprinkle the sea bream with salt and let stand for 1 hour.

Wash away the salt and remove any small bones with tweezers.

Combine all the MARINADE ingredients and soak the sea bream until it turns white (about 5 minutes), remove, reserving Marinade, and let drain for 1 hour.

Wrap the sea bream in the kelp (left over from making bonito stock) and then in plastic wrap and refrigerate for 12 hours.

Prepare the mackerel in the same way, but let it stand about 2 hours covered with salt.

Make the SUSHI DRESSING (page 104).

Wash the rice thoroughly and let stand for 30–60 minutes (page 101).

TO MAKE

Cook the rice (page 101).

Turn the hot cooked rice out into a large wooden bowl and gradually add ⅔ cup (160 ml) Sushi Dressing (or slightly less to taste), mixing well by slicing across the rice with a rice paddle or thin wooden spoon (page 104). Let cool to body temperature, then mound rice in center and cover bowl with a damp cloth.

Make a lengthwise incision down the center of the sea bream to half its thickness. Insert the knife and cut to the right to open the fillet. Repeat with the left side.

Working from the head end of the mackerel fillet, use your hands to pull off the translucent covering. Pare off the thickest part of the fillet to make 2 pieces of fairly equal thickness.

Soak a kitchen cloth in the HAND VINEGAR and wring it out well. Lay the cloth on a bamboo rolling mat and place the open piece of sea bream on the cloth, skin side down and tail end toward you. Moisten your hands with the Hand Vinegar and shape ¾ cup unpacked sushi rice into a rough, loosely packed log about 1½ inches (4 cm) in diameter, then shape into a bar. The rice must be worked, almost kneaded, so it will hold its shape. Place the bar on the fish and wrap the damp cloth and the bamboo rolling mat around it. Press to finish packing the rice and forming the bar.

Place a mackerel fillet (again skin side down) on the bamboo mat as shown and use the smaller slice to fill in around the tail to make a rough rectangle of fish. Use 1½ cups unpacked sushi rice and follow the procedure for the sea bream, making a log of rice approximately 2–2½ inches (5–6 cm) in diameter.

Unwrap the sushi and score the top of the mackerel with decorative shallow cuts.

Cut the bars into ¾-inch (1½-cm) wide slices and arrange on dishes. Garnish with mounds of well-drained sweet-vinegared ginger and serve.

540 Cals

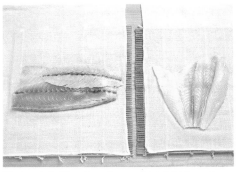
Mackerel (left) and sea bream (right) laid out for rolling

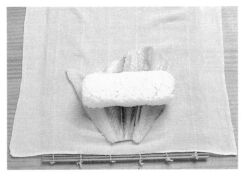
Place bar of rice across fish

Roll fish and rice in bamboo mat and press to shape

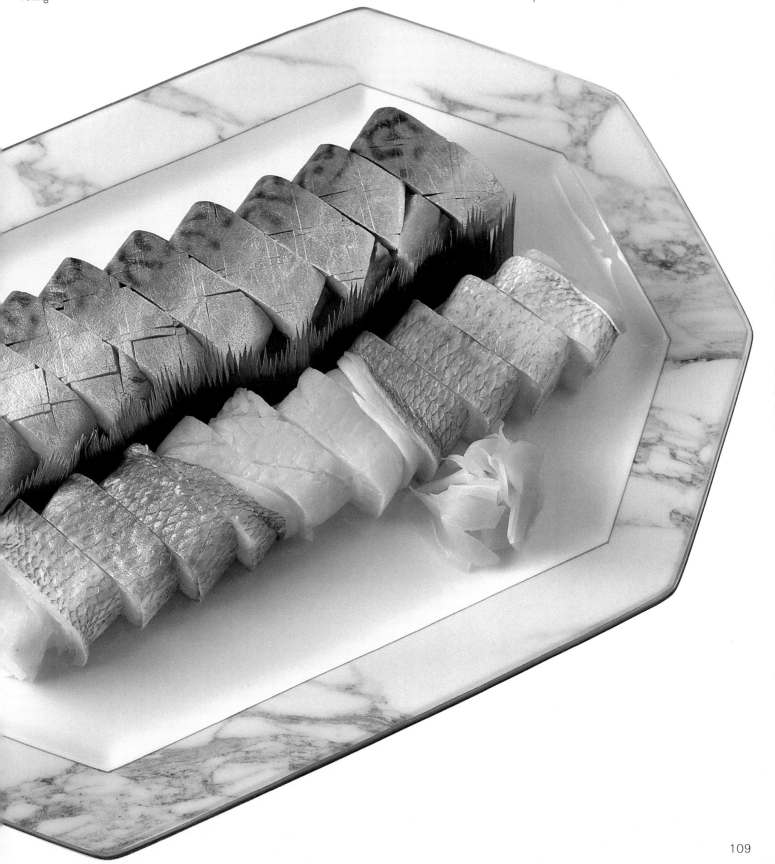

Nigiri Sushi

Nigiri-zushi

Perhaps the most famous of all Japanese foods, Nigiri Sushi is actually relatively new, having been conceived only a little less than two hundred years ago. Some changes have since been made, but essentially Nigiri Sushi remains bite-sized morsels of fish and other foods laid on top of tiny hand-shaped beds of sushi rice. Absolutely fresh topping ingredients and rice just firm enough to hold together but loose enough so that it crumbles as if by itself when eaten are the marks of expertly made Nigiri Sushi.

Serves 4–6 (makes about 80 pieces)

6 oz (180 g) mackerel fillet, with skin

4 sillago, 1 oz (30 g) each, scaled and gutted (optional)

4¼ cups (725 g) uncooked short-grain rice plus 5½ cups (1.3 L) water

8 raw shrimp, 1 oz (25 g) each

6 oz (180 g) belly of tuna fillet (*toro*)

6 oz (180 g) cleaned and skinned squid (page 141)

6 oz (180 g) sea bream or white-fleshed fish fillet

6 oz (180 g) yellowtail fillet

6 oz (180 g) grilled eel (page 145)

⅕ Thick Omelette (page 10)

wasabi horseradish

2 sheets *nori* seaweed

4 oz (120 g) sea urchin

sweet-vinegared ginger (*amazu-shoga*)

MARINADE

2 cups (480 ml) rice vinegar

⅔ cup (160 ml) water

2 Tbsps sugar

2-inch (5-cm) length kelp (*konbu*)

SUSHI DRESSING (see Note, page 105)

¾ cup (180 ml) rice vinegar

8⅓ Tbsps sugar

4 tsps salt

1-inch (3-cm) length kelp (*konbu*)

DIPPING SAUCE

1 cup (240 ml) dark soy sauce

5 tsps *mirin*

HAND VINEGAR

1 cup (240 ml) water plus 2 Tbsps rice vinegar

8 bamboo skewers

TO PREPARE

Sprinkle the mackerel with salt and let stand for 2 hours.

Wash away the salt and remove any small bones with tweezers.

Shape rice into small rectangle

Spread *wasabi* on topping

Place rice on topping and press

Press sides

Turn and press top

Finish shaping

Combine all the MARINADE ingredients and soak the mackerel until it turns white (about 5 minutes), remove, reserving Marinade, and let drain for 1 hour.

Wrap the mackerel in the kelp (left over from making bonito stock) and then in plastic wrap and refrigerate for 12 hours.

Make the SUSHI DRESSING (page 104).

Make the DIPPING SAUCE: Combine the soy sauce and *mirin* in a saucepan, bring slowly to a boil over low heat, skimming constantly, simmer for 2–3 minutes after it reaches the boiling point, then remove from heat and let cool.

Fillet the sillago (page 131), sprinkle lightly with salt, and let stand 40 minutes.

Wash the rice thoroughly and let stand 30–60 minutes (page 101).

Remove the skin from the sillago, place the fillet in the MARINADE for 2–3 minutes, remove, and pat dry.

Skewer the shrimp on the underside from head to tail to prevent curling (page 48) and cook for 3 minutes in lightly salted boiling water, then transfer to ice water. When cool, remove the skewers, shell, and pinch off the head. Slit the underside of the shrimp open and remove the dark vein.

Retrieve the mackerel from the refrigerator, unwrap, and peel off the translucent layer, starting at the head end (page 108).

TO MAKE

Cook the rice (page 101). While the rice is cooking finish other preliminaries.

Cut the tuna, squid, sea bream, yellowtail, and mackerel into $\frac{1}{4} \times 1\frac{1}{2} \times 2\frac{1}{2}$-inch ($\frac{1}{2} \times 4 \times 6$-cm) pieces. There should be about 8 of each.

Reheat the eel over a hot gas flame on a wire rack or in the oven (or follow the directions on the package). Cut into 8 pieces.

Cut the Thick Omelette into $\frac{1}{2} \times \frac{3}{4} \times 2\frac{1}{2}$-inch ($1 \times 2 \times 6$-cm) strips. Slice each strip horizontally in half cutting almost, but not quite, through so that each can be opened (tentlike) to about $\frac{1}{4}$ inch ($\frac{1}{2}$ cm) thick and $1\frac{1}{2}$ inches (4 cm) wide.

When the rice has finished cooking, turn out into a large wooden bowl and combine with 1 cup (or slightly less to taste) Sushi Dressing, mixing well by slicing across the rice with a rice paddle or thin wooden spoon (page 104). Cool with a fan or newspaper to body temperature, then mound rice in center and cover the bowl with a damp cloth.

TO SHAPE

Moisten your hands with HAND VINEGAR. Take a small amount of the sushi rice (about $1\frac{1}{2}$ rounded Tbsps) and cradle it in your right hand at the base of your fingers. Crimp to form a rectangular block about 2–2½ inches

(5–6 cm) long with rounded edges and sides.

Scoop up a very small amount of *wasabi* horseradish with the tip of your finger and spread it on one of the toppings (excluding the sea urchin and Thick Omelette).

Place the shaped rice on top of the *wasabi* and press with the index and middle fingers.

Press and shape the sides, top, and bottom of the sushi, turning as necessary. Repeat, making 8 pieces with each topping, again, excepting the sea urchin and the Thick Omelette.

To make the sea urchin sushi, shape the rice, then ring it with a 1½-inch (4-cm) wide strip of toasted *nori* seaweed (for toasting, see page 143). Press the seaweed against the rice to secure. Season the top of the rice with *wasabi*. Place the sea urchin on top of the rice in the cavity formed by the "walls" of *nori*.

To make the Thick Omelette sushi, shape the rice, place a tented piece of omelette on top, and secure with a thin band of toasted *nori* seaweed. Do not season with *wasabi* horseradish.

Arrange all the finished sushi on a tray or platter and garnish with mounds of the well-drained vinegared ginger. Serve with bowls of dipping sauce.

averages 72 Cals per piece

Thick Roll Sushi

Futo-maki-zushi

A favorite of Osaka, now known and loved throughout Japan, is Thick Roll Sushi, which combines many different simmered ingredients, all wrapped in sushi rice and nori seaweed. Since the freeze-dried tofu, the shiitake mushrooms, and the gourd ribbons are well seasoned during simmering, this is one type of sushi you don't need to dip in any sauce. Nor is it very hard to assemble if you remember to spread the rice without applying pressure.

Serves 4

6 large dried shiitake mushrooms

2 cakes freeze-dried tofu (*Koya-dofu*), about 1 oz (30 g) total

5 yds (5 m) dried gourd ribbons (*kanpyo*) (2 oz/60 g)

2½ cups (425 g) uncooked short-grain rice plus 3¼ cups (780 ml) water

5 stalks green asparagus, trimmed

⅕ Thick Omelette (page 10)

4 sheets *nori* seaweed

sweet-vinegared ginger (*amazu-shoga*)

FOR SIMMERING MUSHROOMS

½ cup (120 ml) water from soaking shiitake mushrooms

½ cup (120 ml) bonito stock (*dashi*) (page 140)

2 Tbsps sugar

2 Tbsps dark soy sauce

FOR SIMMERING TOFU

2 cups (480 ml) bonito stock (*dashi*) (page 140)

3 Tbsps sugar

4 tsps light soy sauce

1 tsp salt

FOR SIMMERING GOURD RIBBONS

2½ cups (600 ml) bonito stock (*dashi*) (page 140)

3½ Tbsps sugar

3 Tbsps light soy sauce

SUSHI DRESSING (see Note, page 105)

½ cup (120 ml) rice vinegar

5½ Tbsps sugar

1½ Tbsps salt

1-inch (2½-cm) length kelp (*konbu*)

HAND VINEGAR

1 cup (240 ml) water plus 2 Tbsps rice vinegar

bamboo rolling mat (page 143)

TO PREPARE

Soak the mushrooms for 6–7 hours (page 142). Reserve soaking water.

Combine the mushrooms, ½ cup (120 ml) of their soaking liquid, and the bonito stock in a saucepan. Cover with a drop-lid (page 143) and bring to a boil over high heat. Reduce heat to low and simmer for 5 minutes. Add the sugar and simmer for another 5 minutes. Season with the soy sauce and simmer until only a small amount of liquid remains in the pan.

Reconstitute the freeze-dried tofu and rinse well (page 81). Place the tofu and its bonito stock in a saucepan, cover with a drop-lid, and bring to a boil over high heat. Reduce the heat to low and simmer for 5 minutes. Add the sugar and simmer for 5 more minutes. Season with the soy sauce and salt and simmer for a final 5 minutes. Remove from heat and let soak to absorb the flavor.

Soften and scrub the gourd ribbons (page 107).

Combine the gourd ribbons and bonito stock in a saucepan, cover with a drop-lid, and bring to a boil over high heat. Reduce the heat to low and simmer for 5 minutes. Add the sugar and simmer for another 5 minutes. Add the soy sauce, simmer for a final 10 minutes, and set aside to soak in the simmering liquid.

Make the SUSHI DRESSING (page 104).

Wash the rice thoroughly and let it drain for 30–60 minutes (page 101).

TO MAKE

Cook the rice (page 101).

Cook the asparagus in lightly salted boiling water until just tender, refresh in cold water, and drain. Quarter lengthwise.

Drain the tofu. Cut it and the Thick Omelette into long ½-inch (1-cm) square spears. Drain the mushrooms and cut into ½-inch (1-cm) wide strips. Drain the gourd ribbons and cut into 8-inch (20-cm) lengths.

Transfer the hot cooked rice to a large wooden bowl and gradually add the Sushi Dressing, mixing well by slicing across the rice with a rice paddle or thin wooden spoon (page 104). Let cool to body temperature, then mound rice in the center and cover bowl with a damp cloth.

Place a sheet of *nori* seaweed on top of a bamboo rolling mat with the shorter end facing you, shiny side down. Wet your fingers with the HAND VINEGAR. Spread 1½ cups unpacked sushi rice over two-thirds of the *nori* seaweed closest to you, using your fingers to spread it evenly.

In the center of the rice make a row of tofu slices. Top the tofu with sliced omelette. Lay out 5–6 strips of the gourd ribbon, then top with sliced mushroom. Add a row of asparagus, alternating the stem and tip ends.

Roll so that the near and far edges of the *rice* meet. When rolling, be sure to hold the rows of ingredients in place with your fingertips. Press the bamboo mat to round and tighten. Make 3 more rolls.

Cut each roll into 8 pieces, each about ¾ inch (1½ cm) wide. Arrange on plates, garnish with mounds of well-drained sweet-vinegared ginger, and serve.

637 Cals

Spread rice evenly without pressing

Lay out ingredients

Roll up, holding ingredients in place

Roll so near and far ends of rice meet

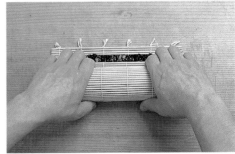
Press mat to firm up and shape roll

Inari Sushi

Inari-zushi

There is something of a legend behind the name Inari Sushi. In Japanese mythology,

Inari was the god of grains, and his messenger was the fox. Now foxes are supposed to be fond of thin deep-fried tofu—just why is lost to history. Still, when it came to stuffing the god's rice grain into pouches of the fox's deep-fried tofu, the name Inari Sushi seemed a natural. The simmered tofu, at once salty and sweet, makes these a favorite, and since the pouches hold their shape better than other sushi, they are quite popular as take-out food.

Serves 4

6 dried shiitake mushrooms

8 ft (2.5 m) dried gourd ribbons (*kanpyo*) (1 oz/30 g)

½ medium carrot

10 pieces thin deep-fried tofu (*usuage*), each 3 inches (8 cm) square

2½ cups (425 g) uncooked short-grain rice plus 3¼ cups (780 ml) water

1 Tbsp white sesame seeds, toasted (page 140)

½ Tbsp black sesame seeds, toasted (page 140)

sweet-vinegared ginger (*amazu-shoga*)

FOR SIMMERING VEGETABLES

1¼ cups (300 ml) bonito stock (*dashi*) (page 140)

½ cup (120 ml) water from soaking shiitake mushrooms

3 Tbsps sugar

1 Tbsp saké

3 Tbsps dark soy sauce

½ tsp salt

FOR SIMMERING TOFU

1⅔ cups (400 ml) bonito stock (*dashi*) (page 140)

3½ Tbsps sugar

5 tsps saké

3 Tbsps dark soy sauce

SUSHI DRESSING (see Note, page 105)

½ cup (120 ml) rice vinegar

5½ Tbsps sugar

1½ Tbsps salt

1-inch (2½-cm) length kelp (*konbu*)

TO PREPARE

Soak the mushrooms for 6-7 hours (page 142). Reserve water.

Soften and scrub the gourd ribbons (page 107).

Dice the mushrooms, gourd ribbons, and carrot into small ⅛-inch (¼-cm) cubes. Boil the carrot until just tender, refresh in cold water, and drain.

Simmer the vegetables: Combine in a saucepan with bonito stock and ½ cup (120 ml) water from soaking, cover with a drop-lid (page 143), and bring to a boil over high heat. Reduce heat to low and simmer for 5 minutes. Add the sugar and saké and simmer for 5 more minutes. Add the soy sauce and

salt and continue simmering until the liquid is almost completely boiled away.

Boil the thin deep-fried tofu for 3 minutes to remove any excess oil. Drain well. Combine the tofu and bonito stock, cover with a drop-lid, and bring to a boil over high heat. Reduce the heat to low and simmer for 5 minutes. Add the sugar and saké and simmer for 5 more minutes. Add the soy sauce and simmer for a final 5 minutes. Remove from heat and let the tofu soak in the liquid.

Make the SUSHI DRESSING (page 104).

Wash the rice thoroughly and let it drain for 30-60 minutes (page 101).

TO MAKE

Cook the rice (page 101).

Turn the hot rice out into a wooden bowl. Add the Sushi Dressing gradually, mixing well by slicing across the rice with a rice paddle or a thin wooden spoon (page 104). Let cool to body temperature.

Add the diced vegetables (reserve pan liquid) and sesame seeds to the sushi rice and mix well. Add about 2 Tbsps of the reserved liquid from cooking the vegetables and again mix thoroughly.

Drain the tofu and cut each square into 2 triangles. Open each triangle along the cut edge to make a small pouch.

Take a portion of rice and form into a loose ball. Stuff into the pouch, then fold the edges of the pouch over the rice.

Arrange on plates and serve garnished with well-drained sweet-vinegared ginger.

929 Cals

Cut tofu squares into triangles

Carefully open up tofu from cut side

Noodles

Chilled *Somen* Noodles

Hiyashi somen

Japanese summers can be unbearably hot, and during the months of July and August especially, it's hard to work up much of an appetite for hot or heavy foods. For that reason, noodles are often served cold. Of the many types of noodles by far the most preferred are the fine, threadlike somen noodles. No summer in Japan would be complete without chilled somen. Texture is all-important with this simple dish, so be sure to use a full pot of water and not to overboil the noodles—there should still be some "bite" left to them.

Serves 4

4 dried shiitake mushrooms
4 eggs
4 raw shrimp, 1 oz (30 g) each
2 oz (60 g) corn salad, trimmed
6 oz (180 g) dried *somen* noodles

FOR SIMMERING MUSHROOMS

⅔ cup (160 ml) bonito stock (*dashi*) (page 140)
3½ Tbsps water from soaking shiitake mushrooms
2 Tbsps sugar
2 Tbsps dark soy sauce

DIPPING SAUCE

2 oz (60 g) dried small shrimp (*hoshi ebi*)
1¼ cups (300 ml) bonito stock (*dashi*) (page 140)
7 Tbsps dark soy sauce
7 Tbsps *mirin*

CONDIMENTS

6 Tbsps finely chopped and rinsed scallion
1 Tbsp finely grated fresh ginger

kitchen thermometer
4 bamboo skewers

TO PREPARE

Soak the mushrooms for 6–7 hours (page 142). Reserve soaking water.

Combine the softened mushrooms, bonito stock, and 3½ Tbsps soaking liquid in a saucepan, cover with a drop-lid (page 143), and bring to a boil over high heat. Reduce heat to low and simmer for 5 minutes. Add the sugar and simmer for another 5 minutes. Add the soy sauce, then simmer for a final 5 minutes. Remove from heat and let the mushrooms cool in the liquid.

TO MAKE

Make 4 Coddled Eggs (page 69). When they are cooked, transfer unshelled eggs to cold water and set aside.

Make the DIPPING SAUCE: Blanch the dried shrimp in boiling water and let drain. Combine the bonito stock, soy sauce, and *mirin* in a saucepan, add the dried shrimp, and bring to a boil over high heat. Cool.

Skewer each shrimp on the underside from head to tail (page 48) and boil in lightly salted water for 3 minutes. Drop in water to cool, then remove skewers and shell, leaving the tail intact. Slit open the underside, remove the dark vein along the back, and cut in half crosswise at a slight angle.

Boil the corn salad in lightly salted water until just tender, refresh in cold water, drain, and gently wring out excess water.

Cook the *somen* noodles until *al dente* (about 2 minutes) according to the directions for *udon* noodles (in the following recipe). Watch them carefully—they cook quickly. Be sure to rinse well but gently to remove starch.

Soak the noodles in ice water to chill.

TO SERVE

Slice the mushrooms into thin strips.

Drain the well-chilled noodles and arrange in serving bowls.

Crack the eggs into cold water and separate the yolk from the white (page 97). Place the yolk on top of the noodles.

Top the noodles with corn salad leaves, shrimp, and mushroom. Serve individual bowls of dipping sauce, which diners season to taste with scallion and ginger.

318 Cals

Udon Pot

Udon suki

The Japanese are quite fond of one-pot cook-ery. One of these cooked-at-the-table spe-cialties is this pot of thick udon noodles with chicken, shellfish, and vegetables all sim-mered in a light broth. A deep electric skillet is ideal for this hearty dish, but a flameproof casserole set on a gas-flame tabletop unit works just as well.

Serves 4

4 live hard-shell clams, no more than 3 oz (90 g) each

1 lb (450 g) dried *udon* noodles

10 oz (300 g) boned chicken thigh

8 raw shrimp, 1 oz (30 g) each, shelled and deveined (page 48)

8 leaves Chinese cabbage

4 1-inch (3-cm) pieces rice cake (*mochi*) (optional)

5 oz (150 g) spinach

½ medium carrot

12 snow peas

4 fresh shiitake mushrooms, washed and stems removed, or 4 fresh brown mush-rooms, washed and trimmed

CONDIMENTS

¾ cup finely chopped and rinsed scallion

4 Tbsps Red Maple Radish (page 140)

2 Tbsps finely grated fresh ginger

4 lemon wedges

BROTH

1¾ qts (1.6 L) bonito stock (*dashi*) (page 140)

⅔ cup (160 ml) light soy sauce

2 Tbsps *mirin*

bamboo rolling mat (page 143)

TO PREPARE

Buy only fresh clams that close tightly when touched. Check the shells for cracks or chips.

Let the clams sit in salted water (1 tsp salt to 3 cups [700 ml] water) in a cool, dark place for 5–6 hours to allow them to expel sand.

TO MAKE

To cook the noodles, bring an ample amount of water—at least 3 qts (3 L)—to a rolling boil and add the noodles. Cook the noodles to *al dente* (tender but still firm to the bite), stirring occasionally to keep them from sticking. When the water returns to a boil, add ½ cup (120 ml) cold water to "firm up" the noodles. Add cold water once more dur-ing cooking. When the noodles are done, remove to a colander and drain, then transfer to a large bowl of cold water and rinse in ample cold running water. When they are

118

cool enough to handle, rub by hand to remove any remaining starch. Drain well. (Dried *udon* noodles cook in 15–20 minutes depending on the thickness and brand.)

Cut the chicken into bite-sized pieces.

Blanch the shrimp in boiling water just until they turn pink, then transfer to cold water and drain.

Parboil the Chinese cabbage, drain, sprin-kle lightly with salt, and let cool. Pare away the thick part of the vein (page 126). Place 2 leaves on a bamboo rolling mat so that the longer edges overlap at the center and the tip of 1 leaf points to the right and the tip of the other to the left (page 127). Roll up the leaves, squeeze out any water by pressing the mat, unroll the mat, and cut rolled leaves into 1-inch (2½-cm) lengths.

Grill the rice cake on a wire net over high heat until it begins to brown slightly (or parch both sides in a dry frying pan until the surface scorches).

Parboil the spinach in lightly salted water and then soak in cold water for 10 minutes. Drain, gently wring out any excess water, and cut the spinach into 1½-inch (4-cm) lengths.

Cut the carrot into ¼-inch (½-cm) thick rounds, boil in lightly salted water until just tender, refresh in cold water, and drain.

String the snow peas, blanch in lightly salted water, refresh in cold water, and drain. Score the mushroom caps (as shown), if desired.

Arrange all the ingredients on large serv-ing platters and place on the table. Set out the condiments.

Combine the BROTH ingredients in a deep electric skillet over high heat. Bring to a boil, reduce heat to medium, and add some of each ingredient. Simmer until ingredients are tender (or heated).

Provide each diner with a bowl. When the food is done, each diner chooses his or her own favorites. Ladle some broth into the bowl and season with condiments to taste.

Restock the skillet with food from the platters as desired.

902 Cals

Soba Noodles in a Basket

Zaru soba

"Simple is best" surely applies to soba, as most connoisseurs agree that the noodles are at their best served at room temperature with a simple sauce.

Serves 4

10 oz (300 g) dried *soba* noodles
1 sheet *nori* seaweed

DIPPING SAUCE

1¼ cups (300 ml) bonito stock (*dashi*) (page 140)
½ cup (120 ml) dark soy sauce
¼ cup (60 ml) *mirin*
1 tsp sugar
¼ cup loose bonito flakes (⅙ oz/5 g)

CONDIMENTS

4 Tbsps finely chopped and rinsed scallion
2 Tbsps grated daikon radish

Udon Noodles with Deep-Fried Tofu

Kitsune udon

Udon noodles are enjoyed in many ways in Japan, but by far the most common is the simplest—a quick bowl of noodles in hot, seasoned broth. Countless variations play upon this theme, for almost anything can be added on top—from a raw egg to a piece of tempura.

Serves 4

4 pieces thin deep-fried tofu (*usuage*), 3 inches (8 cm) square
¾ lb (340 g) dried *udon* noodles
4 scallions, finely slivered
ground red pepper

FOR SIMMERING TOFU

1 cup (240 ml) bonito stock (*dashi*) (page 140)
1½ Tbsps sugar
1 Tbsp saké
1 Tbsp dark soy sauce

BROTH

6½ cups (1.6 L) bonito stock (*dashi*) (page 140)
2 Tbsps dark soy sauce
2 Tbsps light soy sauce
1 Tbsp sugar
⅓ tsp salt

wasabi horseradish
4 quail eggs (optional)

Combine all the DIPPING SAUCE ingredients in a soup pot, except the bonito flakes, and bring to a boil over high heat. Add the bonito flakes, immediately remove from heat, and strain to clarify (page 142).

Cook the *soba* noodles until *al dente* (6–7 minutes), following the directions for *udon* noodles (page 118). Cool.

While the noodles are boiling, toast the *nori* seaweed over a high gas flame (if it has not been pretoasted), then crumble (page 143).

Be sure to drain the noodles well. Divide among 4 bowls and top with *nori* seaweed. Serve with individual bowls of the dipping sauce. Season the sauce to taste with condiments.

324 Cals

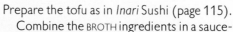

Prepare the tofu as in *Inari* Sushi (page 115).

Combine the BROTH ingredients in a saucepan and bring to a boil over high heat, then reduce heat to very low and simmer for 10 minutes. Set aside. ↗

Cook the *udon* noodles (page 118).

Transfer 1 portion of the noodles to a colander and dip in a pot of hot water to warm to serving temperature. Drain and place in serving bowl. Repeat with remaining portions.

Reheat the broth. Reheat the tofu in simmering liquid. Top the noodles with the tofu and scallion, ladle hot broth into each bowl, and sprinkle with red pepper as desired.

473 Cals

Soba Noodles with Duck

Kamo nanba soba

While some connoisseurs claim that eating plain, cold soba noodles with a simple dipping sauce is the only way to appreciate the noodles' full buckwheat flavor, an equally popular way to eat soba is in a bowl of hot broth.

Serves 4

10 oz (300 g) duck breast
8 scallions
¾ lb (340 g) dried *soba* noodles
ground *sansho* pepper

BROTH

6½ cups (1.6 L) bonito stock (*dashi*) (page 140)
2 Tbsps dark soy sauce
2 Tbsps light soy sauce
1 Tbsp sugar
⅓ tsp salt

Trim any excess fat from the duck breast and reserve. Cut the meat into ¼-inch (½-cm) thick slices.

Cut the scallions into 1½-inch (4-cm) lengths. Heat the duck fat in a frying pan, add the scallions, and sauté lightly. Set aside.

Combine the BROTH ingredients in a saucepan and bring to a boil, then reduce heat to low and simmer for 10 minutes. Add the sliced duck and continue cooking until heated through—about 1 minute. Set aside.

Cook the *soba* noodles until *al dente* (6–7 minutes) following the directions for *udon* noodles (page 118).

Transfer 1 portion of the noodles to a colander, dip in a pot of hot water to warm to serving temperature, and drain. Place in serving bowl. Repeat with remaining portions.

Reheat the broth and duck. Top the noodles with duck meat and scallions. Ladle broth into each bowl and sprinkle with *sansho* pepper as desired.

421 Cals

One-pot Dishes

Sukiyaki

The world-renowned dish Sukiyaki actually only appeared on the horizon of Japanese cuisine some one hundred years ago. Up until then, Buddhist sentiments kept most Japanese from eating pork, beef, and other meats. In fact, it was only after they saw Westerners in Japan cheerfully eating meat that they defied the taboo—and even then with certain misgivings. It seems they could not bring themselves to "taint" kitchen pots and pans, yet somehow instead contrived to use the broad blade of the Japanese plow, or suki, for a grill. From such humble beginnings, Sukiyaki has grown to become the representative beef cuisine of Japan.

Grease heated skillet with beef suet

Sauté beef

Add sauce

Serves 4

2 lbs (900 g) well-marbled sirloin beef
1 cake *konnyaku*, about ½ lb (220 g)
½ block regular ("cotton") tofu, about 5 oz (150 g)
12 scallions
4 oz (120 g) watercress
8 fresh shiitake mushrooms, washed and stems removed, or 8 fresh brown mushrooms, washed and trimmed
2 oz (60 g) beef suet
4 eggs

SAUCE

1 cup (240 ml) dark soy sauce
1 cup (240 ml) *mirin*
½ cup (120 ml) water
7 Tbsps sugar
¼ cup (60 ml) saké

Slice the beef as thinly as possible or have the butcher cut it for Sukiyaki.

Combine all the SAUCE ingredients and bring to a boil over high heat. Cool.

Cut the *konnyaku* into ¼ × ¼ × 2-inch (½ × ½ × 5-cm) strips. Rub with salt, boil for 5 minutes, and drain well (page 142).

Cut the tofu into 8 equal pieces, and the scallions into 1½-inch (4-cm) lengths. Remove the tough stems from the watercress. Cut the mushroom caps in half.

Arrange all the ingredients through mushrooms on a large platter.

Heat a deep electric skillet (at the table) or a cast-iron skillet on a hot plate to high and melt the beef suet, moving it around to grease the whole cooking surface. Add some of the beef to the pot and sauté it. When the beef is almost cooked through, pour in the sauce to the ½-inch (1-cm) level and add some of the *konnyaku*, tofu, and vegetables. Let the food simmer, adjusting heat if necessary.

Break the raw eggs into individual serving bowls and beat lightly.

When the food is cooked through, each diner selects his or her own pieces from the skillet. Dip into the egg.

Replace the ingredients and sauce as they are depleted.

959 Cals

122

Oden Stew
Oden nabe

Chicken, beef, eggs, thick deep-fried tofu, and konnyaku are among the many ingredients simmered for long hours in lightly seasoned chicken broth for this hearty winter "stew." Spicy hot yellow Japanese mustard and ground red pepper are the preferred condiments for giving zest to the broth; pass the mustard around and let each person add to taste. Oden goes well with saké, so it is a familiar sight at drinking spots—the customers ordering Oden by the piece, a plate at a time with each round of drinks. You, too, may wish to linger over Oden, with your favorite beverage in hand. If so, bring the Oden, which stands up to a lengthy simmering, to the table and keep it heated on a hotplate or other tabletop heating unit, picking out the seasoned morsels at a leisurely pace.

Serves 4

1 cake *konnyaku*, about ½ lb (220 g)

4 blocks thick deep-fried tofu (*atsuage*), about 10 oz (300 g) total

10 oz (300 g) beef tendons or shank or shortplate

14 oz (400 g) boned chicken thigh

2 potatoes, 10 oz (300 g) each, peeled and boiled

4 hard-boiled eggs

hot yellow mustard (*karashi*) or any mustard that is not sweet or vinegary

ground red pepper

FISH-PASTE DUMPLINGS

vegetable oil for deep-frying

14 oz (400 g) white-fleshed fish fillet such as flounder, turbot, or halibut

14 oz (400 g) raw shrimp, shelled and deveined (page 48)

2 egg whites

½ tsp salt

FOR SIMMERING

2 qts (2 L) chicken stock (page 22)

1 cup (240 ml) light soy sauce

7 Tbsps saké

7 Tbsps *mirin*

3 Tbsps sugar

1 tsp salt

TO PREPARE

Make the FISH-PASTE DUMPLINGS: Preheat the oil to a low deep-frying temperature (330° F/ 165° C). Place the fish and shrimp in a food processor and whir to mince, add the egg whites and salt, and whir to a smooth paste. Wet your hands and form the paste into cylinders about 2 inches (5 cm) long and 1 inch (2 cm) in diameter. (Makes 16–20.) Deep-fry for 5 minutes or until golden brown. Drain in a colander, then douse with boiling water to remove remaining oil.

Cut the *konnyaku* into 4 triangles. Score in a diamond pattern. Rub with salt, boil for 5 minutes, then drain and let cool (page 142).

Boil the tofu for 3 minutes to remove excess oil, then drain and cut in half.

Cut the beef into bite-sized pieces, blanch briefly in boiling water, refresh in cold water, and drain.

Cut the chicken thigh into 2-inch (5-cm) squares, parboil briefly until the surface of the meat turns white, then drop in cold water. Drain.

Cut each boiled potato into 2–3 pieces. Shell the hard-boiled eggs.

TO MAKE

Combine 1½ qts (1½ L) chicken stock and all the remaining SIMMERING ingredients in a saucepan, add the beef, and bring to a boil over high heat.

Place all the other ingredients, except the mustard and pepper, in a large soup pot. Pour in simmering liquid to cover, place a drop-lid (page 143) over all, and bring to a boil over high heat. Reduce the heat to *very low* and simmer slowly for 2 hours. As the liquid boils away during cooking, occasionally add more chicken stock to make up the difference.

Bring the *Oden* to the table in the pot and let each diner choose his or her own portion. Serve with mustard and ground red pepper.

1109 Cals

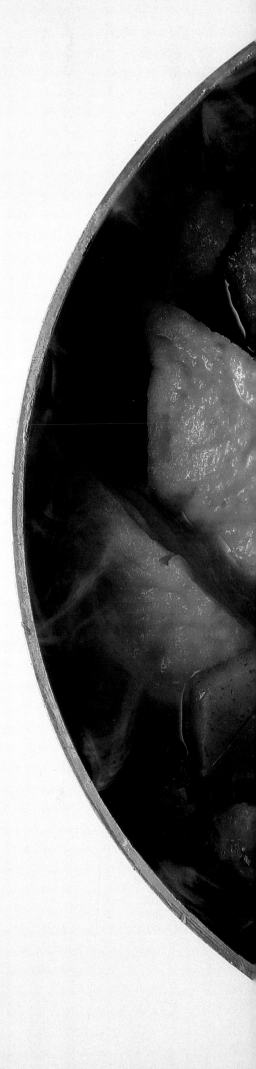

125

Seafood Pot

Yose nabe

The Japanese name for this dish translates literally as "thrown-together pot." As this suggests, the possibilities are endless, so use whatever is on hand. Ingredients are added bit by bit, starting with those having the richer flavor, and are eaten as soon as they are heated through. Green vegetables should be eaten just when they begin to wilt.

Serves 4

8 live hard-shell clams, no more than 3 oz (90 g) each
8 leaves Chinese cabbage
4 oz (120 g) snow peas (about 40)
8 raw shrimp, 1 oz (30 g) each
⅔ oz (20 g) cellophane noodles (*harusame*)
½ lb (220 g) boned chicken thigh
1 lb (450 g) sea bream or sea bass fillets
1 lb (450 g) Spanish mackerel or yellowtail fillets
1 block regular ("cotton") tofu, about 10 oz (300 g)
2 white long onions or 4–6 scallions
5 oz (150 g) watercress
8 fresh shiitake mushrooms, washed and stems removed, or 8 fresh brown mushrooms, washed and trimmed

STOCK

2 qts (2 L) bonito stock (*dashi*) (page 140)
½ cup (120 ml) light soy sauce
7 Tbsps *mirin*
1½ tsps salt

CONDIMENTS

¾ cup finely chopped and rinsed scallion
2 Tbsps Red Maple Radish (page 140)
2 Tbsps grated fresh ginger
4 lemon wedges
ground red pepper

bamboo rolling mat (page 143)

TO PREPARE

When buying clams, choose only those that shut tightly when touched. Avoid ones with chipped or cracked shells.

Place the clams in ample salted water (1½ tsps salt to 3 cups water) and let stand in a cool, dark place for 5–6 hours to allow them to expel sand.

TO MAKE

Parboil the Chinese cabbage, then drain. Sprinkle lightly with salt and cool. Pare away the thick part of the center vein. Lay 2 leaves on a bamboo mat so that they overlap lengthwise, then roll up. Gently press out excess water, remove from mat, and cut into 1-inch (3-cm) lengths.

String the snow peas, parboil in lightly salted water, refresh in cold water, and drain.

Devein the shrimp (page 48) and drop in boiling water until they turn pink (about 3 minutes). Transfer to cold water. When cool, pinch off the heads and remove shells.

Soak the cellophane noodles in lukewarm water to soften, then cut into 4-inch (10-cm) lengths.

Cut the boned chicken into 1-inch (3-cm) squares.

Slice the fish at a slight angle into ½ × 2-inch (1 × 5-cm) pieces.

Cut the tofu into 8 equal pieces, and the onions into 1½-inch (4-cm) lengths. Remove the tough stems from the watercress.

Combine all the STOCK ingredients in a soup pot and bring to a boil over high heat.

TO SERVE

Arrange all the ingredients through mushrooms attractively on large platters. Bring to the table. Set out a bowl for each diner.

Heat the stock in a deep electric skillet (at the table). Add some fish, shellfish, and vegetables.

Trim thick vein

When foods are heated through, let each diner choose food from the pot. Ladle some broth over the food and season to taste with condiments. Refill with fresh food from the platter as the supply in the pot decreases.

734 Cals.

Lay cabbage leaves on mat so they overlap slightly, then roll

Other Delectables

Savory Pancake
Okonomi-yaki

Savory "As-You-Like-It" Pancakes, as the Japanese name has it, are just that: after the obligatory flour, egg, and shredded cabbage, all other ingredients—pork, beef, shrimp, squid, whatever—are left up to personal preference. At specialty restaurants and snack bars that have tables with built-in griddles, each person becomes a chef, in charge of cooking his or her own pancake.

Serves 4

½ large head cabbage, about 1¼ lbs (600 g)

8 raw shrimp, 1 oz (25 g) each, shelled and deveined (page 48)

½ lb (220 g) squid, cleaned and skinned (page 141)

2 cups (240 g) flour

½ tsp baking powder

4 pinches salt

4 eggs

4 Tbsps *tenkasu* (deep-fried tempura batter crumbs; optional)

2 Tbsps vegetable oil

10 oz (300 g) pork belly, thinly sliced

2 Tbsps finely chopped red vinegared ginger (*beni-shoga*)

hot yellow mustard (*karashi*) or any mustard that is not sweet or vinegary

TOPPINGS

Okonomi-yaki Sauce (see Note)

mayonnaise

dried bonito powder (*ko-gatsuo*) or dried
  bonito flakes

green-seaweed flakes (*ao-nori*)

Chop the cabbage coarsely. Cut the shrimp in half lengthwise. Cut the squid into ¼ × ¼ × 1½-inch (½ × ½ × 4-cm) spears.

Divide all the ingredients through *tenkasu* into 4 portions and mix to make 4 separate bowls of cake batter: Combine the flour (½ cup [60 g] per pancake), baking powder, ¼ cup (60 ml) water, and pinch salt in a bowl and then mix in the chopped cabbage. Add the egg and mix well. Finally add the squid, shrimp, and *tenkasu* and mix again.

Coat the bottom of a large frying pan with vegetable oil and sauté one-quarter of pork briefly over high heat. Reduce heat to medium, pour 1 bowl of batter in over the pork and shape into a round pancake about 1 inch (2 cm) thick and 8 inches (20 cm) in diameter. Top with the red vinegared ginger and cook until the bottom begins to brown—the center should still be somewhat loose. Turn and brown the other side.

When cooked through, brush on a generous coating of *Okonomi-yaki* Sauce and mayonnaise and sprinkle with bonito powder (or flakes) and green-seaweed flakes. Transfer to a plate and serve with mustard. Make 3 more cakes, serving each as soon as it is done.

920 Cals

NOTE: If *Okonomi-yaki* Sauce is not available, make the following substitute. Combine 2 Tbsps tomato puree, 2 Tbsps ketchup, ⅓ cup (80 ml) Worcestershire sauce, 3 Tbsps dark soy sauce, 1 tsp sugar, and 7 Tbsps bonito stock (*dashi*; page 140) in a saucepan and bring to a boil over high heat. Thicken with 2 Tbsps cornstarch dissolved in 2 Tbsps water, return to a boil, remove from heat, and let cool.

Tempura

Although tempura is famous worldwide as a thoroughly Japanese dish, its origins seem to lie with the fried foods that Portuguese or Spanish missionaries brought to Japan.

The very best tempura adds only the thinnest, crispiest coating to absolutely fresh ingredients, but often when preparing tempura toppings for rice or noodles more batter is used for greater volume (see Vegetable-and-Shrimp Clusters, page 87). Practiced chefs vary the oil temperature and the thickness of the batter to match different ingredients. Here, though, is a shorter, foolproof method.

Serves 4

½ medium sweet potato
8 raw shrimp, 1 oz (25 g) each
5 oz (150 g) squid

4 sillago (*kisu*), 1 oz (30 g) each, or 5 oz (150 g) flounder, turbot, or halibut fillet
4 shucked scallops, 2 oz (60 g) each
½ lb (220 g) winter squash
4 fresh shiitake mushrooms, washed and stems removed, or 4 fresh brown mushrooms, washed and trimmed
4 mint leaves, trimmed
vegetable oil for deep-frying
flour
juice from 1 lemon

DIPPING SAUCE

1¼ cups (300 ml) bonito stock (*dashi*) (page 140)
5 Tbsps dark soy sauce
5 Tbsps *mirin*
¼ cup loose bonito flakes (⅙ oz/5 g)

BATTER

2 egg yolks
1⅔ cups (400 ml) ice water
1⅔ cups (200 g) sifted flour

CONDIMENTS

1 cup grated daikon radish or white radish
2 tsps finely grated fresh ginger

TO PREPARE

Ready ingredients for deep-frying.

Potato: Peel and slice into ¼-inch (½-cm) rounds. Soak in water for 10 minutes. Drain and pat dry.

Shrimp: Remove the head and devein (page 48). Shell, leaving the tail intact. Make several shallow cuts across the underside of each shrimp so that they lie flat. Cut off

the tip of the tail and force out any moisture with the dull side of a knife.

Squid: Clean (page 141), then score each side in a shallow diamond pattern. Cut into 1-inch (3-cm) squares.

Fish: For the sillago, scale, cut off the head, and remove the entrails. Wash well and wipe dry. Slit from head to tail along the vertebrae to remove the top fillet. Discard the backbone (the tail should come with it), then remove the small bones from the abdomen area of both fillets. If using flounder or other fillets, check for any small bones, then cut into bite-sized pieces.

Scallops: Remove any membrane or tough white muscle so that only the soft, fleshy disc remains. Cut each scallop into 2 or 3 thin coinlike slices. Score each side in a shallow diamond pattern.

Winter squash: Seed, then peel away most of the skin in strips, leaving some as decoration. Cut into ¼-inch (½-cm) thick bite-sized slices.

Mushrooms: Cut in half at a slight angle.

Mint: Remove the tough stems.

TO MAKE

Preheat the oil to a medium-low deep-frying temperature (330°–340° F/165°–170° C).

Make the DIPPING SAUCE: Combine the bonito stock, soy sauce, and *mirin* in a saucepan and bring to a boil over high heat. Add the bonito flakes, immediately remove from heat, and strain to clarify (page 142).

Make the BATTER: Combine the egg yolks and ice water in a bowl and mix gently. Add the flour all at once and stir briefly. Batter should be rough and only half mixed, not well mixed and sticky.

Beginning with the vegetables (including the mint leaves), dredge the ingredients one after another in flour, dip in the batter to coat loosely, and deep-fry. Fill no more than one-third the surface in order to maintain a constant oil temperature. Skim the extra batter and debris from the surface of the oil frequently. (Batter crumbs may be used in Savory Pancake, page 128.)

Raise the oil temperature slightly (10°–20° F/5°–10° C) and fry the seafood in the same way.

Line serving plates with absorbent paper and serve the fried pieces as soon as possible. Dip the tempura in sauce seasoned with radish and ginger, or in lemon juice salted to taste.

791 Cals

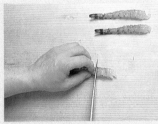
Score underside of shrimp to flatten

Trim tail of shrimp, then force out moisture

Scale, remove head, and gut sillago

Fillet sillago

Combine egg yolk and ice water

Pour in flour all at once and mix roughly

Coat ingredients with flour

Deep-fry, covering no more than one-third of oil surface

131

Deep-Fried Mixed Kebabs

Kushi-katsu

Many specialty restaurants in Japan offer vast menus of these deep-fried breaded kebabs, each establishment boasting a secret sauce or some special selection of skewered ingredients. While the cook at home can't go to equal lengths, there's no reason why you can't improve on the basic recipe to create your own specialties.

Serves 4

SINGLE-ITEM KEBABS

12 live hard-shell clams, 2 oz (60 g) each
4 oz (120 g) beef tenderloin or sirloin
4 oz (120 g) boneless pork loin
4 oz (120 g) boned chicken thigh
3 oz (90 g) white-fleshed fish fillet
4 shucked scallops, 2 oz (60 g) each
4 raw shrimp, 1 oz (30 g) each
3 oz (90 g) squid, cleaned and skinned (page 141)

DOUBLE-ITEM KEBABS

2 oz (60 g) thinly sliced beef
4 stalks green asparagus

4 thin slices pork
1 stalk celery

3 oz (90 g) boned chicken thigh
2 scallions

3 oz (90 g) white-fleshed fish fillet
3 oz (90 g) sea urchin

4 oz (120 g) squid
1 sheet *nori* seaweed

3 oz (90 g) beef tenderloin or sirloin
1 bell pepper

3 oz (90 g) thinly sliced pork
3 oz (90 g) Gruyère cheese

DIPPING SAUCE

⅓ cup (80 ml) Worcestershire sauce
4 Tbsps bonito stock (*dashi*) (page 140)
3 Tbsps dark soy sauce
2 Tbsps tomato puree
2 Tbsps tomato ketchup
1 tsp sugar
hot yellow mustard (*karashi*) or any mustard that is not sweet or vinegary

FOR BREADING

2 eggs
1⅔ cups (400 ml) water
1¼ cups (150 g) sifted flour
½ tsp baking powder

flour (for dredging)
4 cups (300 g) fresh bread crumbs

vegetable oil for deep-frying
juice from 1 lemon

60 bamboo skewers

TO PREPARE

Buy only fresh clams that close tightly when touched (or are already shut tight). Avoid those with cracked or chipped shells.

Place the clams in salted water (1½ tsps salt to 3 cups water) and let stand for 5–6 hours to allow them to expel sand.

TO ASSEMBLE

Make 4 skewers of each SINGLE-ITEM KEBAB.

Clams: Open and clean (page 45). Thread 3 to a skewer.

132

Beef, pork, and chicken: Cut into ½-inch (1½-cm) cubes. Skewer 3–4 cubes of meat on each kebab.

Fish: Cut into 4 equal strips (½ × ½ × 2 inches/1 × 1 × 5 cm). Thread lengthwise, 1 piece per skewer.

Scallops: Remove any membrane or muscle so that only the fleshy disc remains. Cut into ½-inch (1½-cm) cubes. Thread the meat of 1 scallop on 1 skewer.

Shrimp: Shell and devein (page 48), leaving the tail and legs intact. Skewer lengthwise from the tail end.

Squid: Score in a diamond pattern on both sides. Cut into ½-inch (1½-cm) cubes. (If using small squid with thin flesh, cut into ½ × 1½-inch [1½ × 4-cm] strips.) Thread 2 pieces to a skewer.

Make the DOUBLE-ITEM KEBABS, again 4 of each.

Beef and asparagus: Trim the asparagus and roll a single stock up in a thin strip of beef. Cut into 3 pieces. Thread 3 pieces to each skewer.

Pork and celery: String the celery and cut into fine 1½-inch (4½-cm) spears. Wrap several spears with the thinly sliced pork. Cut each roll into ½-inch (1½-cm) rounds. Three rounds make 1 kebab.

Chicken and scallions: Cut the scallions into ½-inch (1½-cm) lengths and the chicken into ½-inch (1½-cm) squares. Thread 2 pieces of each to the skewer, alternating the chicken and scallion.

Fish and sea urchin: Cut the fish into 8 very thin (⅛-inch/¼-cm) slices. Divide the sea urchin into 8 portions. Wrap a slice of fish around 1 portion of sea urchin. Make 4 skewers, 2 rolls to each.

Squid and nori seaweed: If using squid with thick flesh, cut in half horizontally to a thickness of ¼ inch (½ cm). Score one side of the squid in a diamond pattern. Toast the nori seaweed over a high gas flame if it has not been pretoasted (page 143). Cut the nori seaweed to the same size as the squid, lay on unscored side of squid, and roll up. Cut into ½-inch (1-cm) lengths, and skewer 3–4 pieces to a kebab.

Beef and bell pepper: Core and seed the bell pepper, then cut into ½-inch (1½-cm) squares. Cut the beef into ½-inch (1½-cm) cubes. Thread 2–3 pieces of each to a skewer, alternating the beef and pepper.

Pork and cheese: Slice the cheese into 4 equal bars (½ × ½ × 2 inches/1 × 1 × 4 cm), wrap each in a thin slice of pork, and skewer.

Combine all the DIPPING SAUCE ingredients, except the mustard, in a saucepan and bring to a boil over high heat. Remove from heat, stir in mustard to taste, and cool.

TO DEEP-FRY

Preheat the oil to a medium deep-frying temperature (340° F/170° C).

Mix together the eggs and water for the BREADING, sift in the 1¼ cups flour and baking powder, and beat well with a whisk.

Dredge all the skewers lightly in flour, dip in the batter, and roll in bread crumbs.

Deep-fry the skewers, a few at a time, for 2–2½ minutes until golden brown.

Arrange the fried skewers on plates and serve hot. Dip in the sauce or sprinkle with lemon juice and salt. Garnish with raw vegetables if desired.

1635 Cals

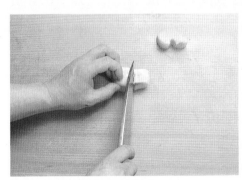

Cut away any tough muscular tissue

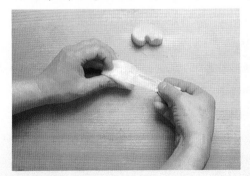

Peel off translucent membrane

Box Meal
Bento

Box Meal

Bento

When the weather turns nice, people everywhere enjoy eating outdoors. In Japan, the changing seasons bring people from all walks of life out to scenic spots to view the cherry blossoms in early spring, followed soon by the azaleas, and later the harvest moon and autumn leaves. There picnickers partake of saké and seasonal foods—and yes, even in this day and age, some Japanese still compose haiku in celebration of the mood.

Of course, the origins of outdoor meal-taking were not necessarily so poetic. The take-along meal owes at least as much to the frugal repasts farmers brought with them to the fields and to the meager provisions foot soldiers carried around on campaigns. Often there was little more than pickles and dried cooked rice—just enough to stave off hunger. With the advent of a leisure culture, people began packing meals for day trips, pleasure excursions, and theater-going. Thus, there developed a wide variety of forms and practices, from the plainest everyday fare in

"throw-away" boxes to fancy preparations aesthetically arranged in decorative containers. Today, bento box meals are usually either for taking to the office or school or for outings and travel. It is now possible to buy the ready-made bento in most train stations, some of which have become famous for their enticing box meals with local delicacies.

The containers have also changed considerably over the years. Nowadays it is not uncommon to use metal or plastic airtight wares or disposable wooden lunch boxes, these last perfect for simmered and rice dishes since they absorb just the right amount of moisture. In times past, however, people might have simply wrapped rice balls and pickles in bamboo-shoot casings or, conversely, used special lacquerware boxes—the most formal of which were quite elaborate affairs, complete with serving dishes and saké sets in one case.

Today, the seasonal events still call for a picnic—and a few common-sense tips will ensure success. Foods to be taken outdoors should be chosen from among those that do not spoil easily or prove unappealing when eaten cold. Nor should they have too much

liquid. With this last in mind, simmered foods should be well drained and hot foods allowed to cool before putting them in a sealed container. The secret is to prepare well-seasoned dishes that will hold up over a number of hours. It is also important to consider what foods go well together in terms of color and taste. Flavors likely to overpower those next to them should be partitioned off by inserting a well-washed odorless leaf. Finally, all available space in the container should be filled, both to make for a more balanced appearance and to prevent undue shifting and settling of the contents.

A combination of Japanese and Western wares has been used for packing the picnic lunch on pages 134-35. On the left-hand side are a Western-style wicker breadbasket and plastic-lidded enamelware containers; on the right, Japanese-style unfinished wood boxes of somewhat sturdier construction than the disposable box. Whatever the containers—from a cozy picnic basket to a formal lacquerware treasure—the memory of the meal and the company will be what lingers long after the day has passed, so choose both with care.

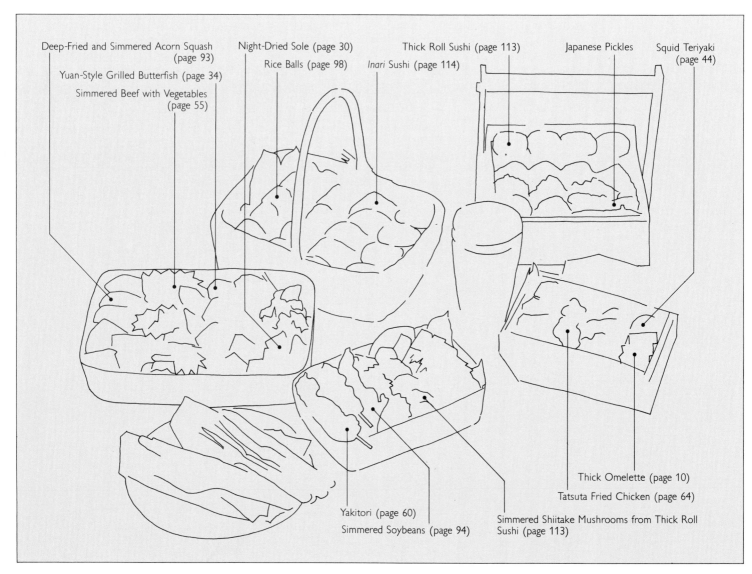

Deep-Fried and Simmered Acorn Squash (page 93)
Yuan-Style Grilled Butterfish (page 34)
Simmered Beef with Vegetables (page 55)
Night-Dried Sole (page 30)
Rice Balls (page 98)
Thick Roll Sushi (page 113)
Inari Sushi (page 114)
Japanese Pickles
Squid Teriyaki (page 44)
Thick Omelette (page 10)
Tatsuta Fried Chicken (page 64)
Simmered Shiitake Mushrooms from Thick Roll Sushi (page 113)
Yakitori (page 60)
Simmered Soybeans (page 94)

Shokado Box Meal

Shokado Bento

At the crossroads of the Japanese sensibilities for miniaturization and appetizing food presentation is the *bento*, the modular "box meal." Coming in a number of types, they have the merit of compactness and present a more-or-less complete course.

The distinctive *Shokado* Box Meal is served at lunch, dinner, and parties in a lidded, square lacquer box partitioned into four sections by a cross-grid inset. Attention is paid to creating a colorful array of food items among the different sections. Small saucers or cups can even be set inside one or more sections as required for dressed or simmered dishes.

The name of the *Shokado* serving box traces back to a certain elder Buddhist priest, Nakanuma Shojo, who adapted a common farmer's seed box for use in holding smoking articles and painting supplies. A painter and calligrapher by avocation—he ranked among the Three Great Calligraphers of the mid-seventeenth century—in his later years he

took up residence in a small thatched hut to lead the aesthetic life. Naming his retreat Shokado, or "Pine-Blossom Hall," he created many works of art under the name Shokado Shojo, no doubt working directly out of his favorite compartmentalized box. It was not until the twentieth century, however, that some inventive and erudite cook hit upon the idea of serving food in such boxes with the allusive name Shokado.

The possibilities for the *Shokado* serving box are virtually limitless. There are no set rules dictating what food is to be arranged in which partitioned section, though most cooks try to present a menu that draws from the various courses of the classic Japanese meal: an appetizer, raw fish, soup (served separately), a grilled or broiled dish, a simmered dish, and rice (here represented by the sushi). Besides the arrangements presented on the following two pages, one might choose to proceed from slices of raw fish in the lower right-hand section to hot rice in the lower left-hand section, with grilled and simmered dishes above, the whole supplemented with a bowl of broth. Another appealing arrangement might be an appetizer

in the lower right, raw fish in the lower left, a grilled food in the upper left, and a simmered dish in the upper right, with hot rice and soup served alongside.

The photograph on the left shows a vermilion lacquerware *Shokado* serving box, but there are many other kinds from the simplest plain wooden ones to those in ornate black lacquer. Furthermore, Western wares work superbly in a *Shokado* format, as can be seen in the serving example in the right-hand photograph. Here a silver tray holds four Italian dishes in an arrangement that echoes the *Shokado* image. For the hors d'oeuvres, five tiny vessels have been arranged on a slightly larger plate, although appetizers without dressing might easily be served directly on a plate the same size as the others. And, of course, according to the occasion, less formal *Shokado*-style presentations can be made using wooden trays or luncheon mats. The key thing to remember is that the cook should always be an artist, too. Try out your own creative sense of composition and design.

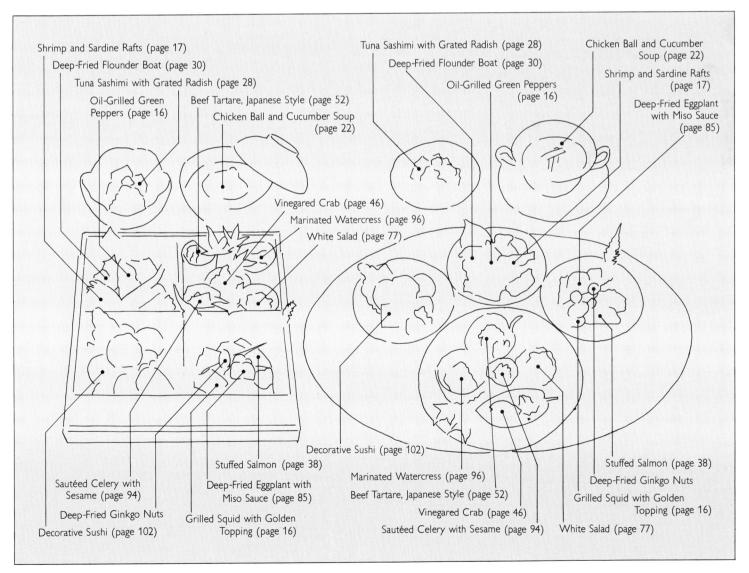

Shrimp and Sardine Rafts (page 17)
Deep-Fried Flounder Boat (page 30)
Tuna Sashimi with Grated Radish (page 28)
Oil-Grilled Green Peppers (page 16)
Beef Tartare, Japanese Style (page 52)
Chicken Ball and Cucumber Soup (page 22)
Vinegared Crab (page 46)
Marinated Watercress (page 96)
White Salad (page 77)

Tuna Sashimi with Grated Radish (page 28)
Deep-Fried Flounder Boat (page 30)
Oil-Grilled Green Peppers (page 16)

Chicken Ball and Cucumber Soup (page 22)
Shrimp and Sardine Rafts (page 17)
Deep-Fried Eggplant with Miso Sauce (page 85)

Sautéed Celery with Sesame (page 94)
Deep-Fried Ginkgo Nuts
Decorative Sushi (page 102)
Stuffed Salmon (page 38)
Deep-Fried Eggplant with Miso Sauce (page 85)
Grilled Squid with Golden Topping (page 16)
Decorative Sushi (page 102)
Marinated Watercress (page 96)
Beef Tartare, Japanese Style (page 52)
Vinegared Crab (page 46)
Sautéed Celery with Sesame (page 94)
Stuffed Salmon (page 38)
Deep-Fried Ginkgo Nuts
Grilled Squid with Golden Topping (page 16)
White Salad (page 77)

Shokado Box Meal
Shokado Bento

COOKING TIPS

BONITO STOCK (dashi)

Makes 6½ cups (1.6 L)

about 20-inch (50-cm) length kelp (konbu) (1½ oz/40 g)
2 qts (2 L) cold water
3 cups loose bonito flakes (2 oz/60 g)

1. Moisten a clean cloth and wring well. Carefully but thoroughly wipe the surface of the kelp. Kelp should never be washed since flavor is lost in the process. Place the cold water and kelp in a soup pot and slowly bring to a boil over a medium-low to medium heat. Regulate the heat so the water takes approximately 10 minutes to reach a boil.

2. When fine bubbles begin to appear at the edges of the pot, press your thumbnail into the thickest part of the seaweed. If it enters easily, the flavor has been properly released. If the kelp is still tough, return to the pot for 1-2 minutes. Do not allow the water to boil while the kelp is in the pot. (Reserve the kelp for wrapping ingredients to infuse flavor, as in Decorative Sushi [page 104]. Kelp keeps 3-4 days if patted dry, covered with plastic wrap, and refrigerated.)

3. When the water boils, add ⅓-½ cup (80-120 ml) cold water.

4. Add the bonito flakes.

5. When the stock returns to a boil, remove it from the heat and skim the surface.

6. When the bonito flakes sink to the bottom (30-60 seconds), strain to clarify (page 142). Do not wring the flakes.

7. The finished stock should be clear and free of any bonito flake particles.

NOTE: Instant bonito stock is a convenient alternative to preparing stock from scratch (see page 146).

SESAME SEEDS

1. To toast, place the sesame seeds in a dry pan over low heat. Shake the pan continually and remove sesame seeds from the pan as soon as they begin to swell and release some oil. The seeds should be a light golden color.

2. To make sesame paste, add larger amounts of toasted seeds to a blender and whir to a coarse paste (or grind smaller amounts by hand in a mortar and pestle).

3. Press paste through a fine drum sieve.

NOTE: Prepared pastes available in oriental markets can be used, but they generally contain ground peanut and lack the aroma and taste that only freshly ground sesame can have.

RED MAPLE RADISH

Makes 6-7 Tbsps

2-3 dried red chili peppers
4-inch (10-cm) length daikon radish (see Note)

1. Chop the top off the chili peppers. Roll each pepper between your fingers, top side down, to force out the seeds.

2. Peel the daikon radish, puncture deeply in several places with an ice pick or chopstick, then force the peppers into the holes. Set aside for 2-3 minutes to allow the chilies to soften.

3. Grate the stuffed daikon over a bamboo rolling mat (page 143) or cheesecloth. Squeeze out some of the moisture.

NOTE: If daikon radish is unavailable, grate white radish and mix in cayenne pepper to taste.

CLEANING SQUID

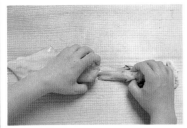

1. Grasp the body sac in one hand and steadily but gently pull the tentacles away from the body. Reach inside the body sac and remove the remaining contents, including the transparent quill.

2. Insert a finger under the fin and disengage it, then pull it off, taking as much skin as possible.

3. Peel off the remaining skin. If it does not come away easily, rub with cheesecloth, then peel. Cut off the tentacles above the eyes. Wash the body (reserve tentacles for other uses) well before proceeding.

GINKGO NUTS

1. Crack the shell open with the back of a knife or a nutcracker.

2. Remove the shells.

3. Blanch the nuts in rapidly boiling water to cover. Roll then with a skimmer to loosen skin.

4. Transfer the nuts to cold water. Peel.

TURNIP CHRYSANTHEMUM

1. Peel the turnip.

2. Cut the turnip horizontally into ¾-inch (2-cm) thick rounds. Score the rounds as finely as possible, then turn 90° and score again, so that you have a fine grid penetrating to at least three-quarters the thickness of the rounds.

3. Turn the rounds over and cut each one into ½-inch (1½-cm) squares. Add the kelp to ample cold salted water (2 tsps salt to 1½ cups [360 ml] water) and soak until turnip becomes tender (about 20 minutes).

4. Stem and seed the chili peppers. Combine the rice vinegar, water, sugar, and salt in a saucepan and bring to a boil over high heat. When the liquid boils, add the chili peppers, then immediately remove pan from heat. Set in a large bowl of ice water and force-cool.

5. Remove the turnip pieces. Press out the excess moisture.

6. Soak the turnip in the rice vinegar marinade for at least 1 hour.

7. Before serving remove the turnip from the marinade, drain, and spread out the "petals" of the flower with your fingers or with chopsticks. Garnish with a thin round of chili pepper.

NOTE: Turnip Chrysanthemums keep 1 week refrigerated if placed in an airtight container with marinade.

SOAKING DRIED SHIITAKE MUSHROOMS

1. Rinse the mushrooms quickly.

2. Place in ample cold water and cover with a drop-lid (see facing page) for 1 hour.

3. Drain.

4. Add fresh water to just cover, replace the drop-lid, and let stand for 5–6 hours to soften.

5. Remove the mushrooms, reserving the soaking water, and cut off stems.

6. If using the soaking liquid, strain to clarify (see below).

SOAKING DRIED CLOUD EAR MUSHROOMS

1. The dried cloud ear will swell to several times its original size when soaked.

2. Place the mushroom(s) in ample cold water, cover with a drop-lid (see facing page), and let stand for 1 hour. Trim.

3. The cloud ear after soaking 1 hour.

PREPARING *KONNYAKU*

1. Cut the *konnyaku* as instructed in the recipe, sprinkle with salt, and then scrub well.

2. Cook the salted *konnyaku* in boiling water for 5 minutes.

3. Drain and cool.

HOW TO STRAIN AND CLARIFY

To strain tiny particles from soups and sauces, use a finely woven material. The best material is undyed cotton flannel. If cotton flannel is not available, a jelly bag or a paper coffee filter are the next-best substitutes. Another possibility is to use a kitchen cloth (non-terry) with a close weave. This or any similar substitute should be folded double before straining liquids.

Before using cotton flannel or any other cloth, rinse and then wring out. After use, wash with a mild dish soap, rinsing thoroughly to remove any residual suds. Dry well before storing.

New cotton flannel should be boiled for 5–10 minutes and soaked for about 20 minutes to remove the odor of the cloth.

SOAKING DRIED *WAKAME* SEAWEED

1. Place the seaweed in ample water, cover with a drop-lid (see below), and let stand for 20 minutes.

2. Drain and then drop in boiling water until the color brightens.

3. Remove and plunge into ice water.

4. Drain and cut away the tough vein.

BAMBOO ROLLING MATS

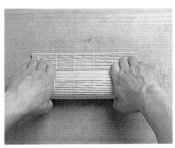

Bamboo rolling mats made of thin bamboo slats woven together with a strong cotton string have a wide range of uses. In Japanese cuisine, they appear most frequently in rolled sushi recipes, but are equally effective for draining and pressing excess liquid from foodstuffs such as grated daikon radish, boiled spinach, or any other material that retains water easily.

Care should be taken when purchasing a bamboo rolling mat. Each of the slats should be round and free of joints. There should be very little space between the slats but what little there is should be equal from left to right and between strips. Mats should be tightly woven. Test this by holding the sides of the open mat with both hands so that the slats run horizontally, then apply tension by moving one hand up and the other down and then reversing the action. Repeat several times. This will reveal any gaps between the slats, as well as any sloppiness in the weaving. You may be tempted by plastic imitations, but they are sensitive to heat and break easily, so search for the authentic article before settling for plastic.

After every use, the mat should be scrubbed with a brush to remove particles of food from between the slats, then stood on end to dry thoroughly before storing in a dry place out of direct sunlight.

TOASTING AND CRUMBLING *NORI* SEAWEED

1. *Nori* seaweed often comes pre-toasted. But if it has not been toasted, it is a simple matter to do so: pass both sides of the seaweed over a hot gas flame until the color brightens and the sheet becomes crisp.

2. To crumble, first tear the seaweed into small pieces.

3. Wrap the small pieces in a dry cheesecloth and then rub to crumble.

DROP-LIDS

These simple but effective devices derive their name from the fact that they are dropped into the cooking vessel to rest directly on the ingredients or liquid inside. Used mainly for simmering, drop-lids ensure even heat and flavor distribution by forcing the rising heat down and the simmering liquid to circulate. Whereas a pot lid only covers, a drop-lid pushes floating ingredients into the pot liquor for even cooking. Resting directly on the food has an additional benefit in that it restricts the movement of solids, and so prevents delicate ingredients from crumbling. From an economic standpoint, it should be noted that drop-lids allow the cook to get by with smaller amounts of sauces, seasonings, and heat, since the foods are forced into the liquid and are done sooner.

Though a wooden drop-lid is recommended, the resourceful cook may improvise with vented parchment paper. Cut it to a diameter slightly larger than the pot it is to be used with, pierce in the center to allow any steam to escape, and then place in the saucepan so the outer edge of the paper presses against the side of the pot and the parchment lies on the food or liquid.

Drop-lids are absorbent, so soak them in water before every use to saturate. If this is not done, they will rob the simmering sauce of some of its flavor and volume. Not only that, but the next time the lid is used it will release the flavors. Boiling the lid after every use is the ideal, but a thorough washing will suffice. The lid should be allowed to dry completely before putting it away in a dry place out of direct sunlight.

Newly purchased wooden drop-lids should be boiled before using them for the first time to remove the smell of the wood.

INGREDIENTS

The number of outlets that carry Japanese foodstuffs continues to rise with each passing year. Where once a long trip to that Japanese market was a prerequisite to procuring authentic ingredients, today a wide range of shops offers numerous products under both American and Japanese brands.

Increased popularity of Japanese cuisine has led to increased availability of many Japanese foodstuffs. Many products that have gained a broad following, such as tofu and miso, now have their own corner in supermarkets, healthfood stores, and gourmet shops. Korean, Chinese, and "Oriental" markets now stock many Japanese products, not to mention foods shared between cuisines like shiitake mushrooms and cellophane noodles (*harusame*). With the popularity of sushi, both *wasabi* horseradish and *nori* seaweed appear to be on their way to becoming household words and supermarket staples; likewise, very fresh or quick-frozen seafood to be eaten as sashimi, or raw, can be found at better fishmongers and markets. Fresh vegetables, most notably daikon radishes and shiitake mushrooms, have also made inroads on the more common outlets.

The following glossary of ingredients offers a visual depiction of all the Japanese ingredients and the less-familiar seafood in this book. All are available in the United States. Storage instructions are included where they are necessary, as are tips for choosing fresh or high-quality foods.

ABALONE

This rather plain-looking mollusk is not only a gourmet's delight but is also widely used in the production of cultured pearls. The crisp, white flesh makes wonderful *sashimi*, and, seasoned with saké and steamed, it is one of the true delicacies of Japanese cuisine. In selecting abalone, keep in mind that the very best are those that are still alive. The flesh should be shiny and should contract when touched. If the body is sagging over the edge of the shell, or if the flesh does not move when touched, it is not fresh. After purchase, clean it as soon as possible and refrigerate in plastic wrap. Abalone must be eaten on the day of purchase.

BAMBOO SHOOTS

The arrival of fresh bamboo shoots each year signals the beginning of spring in Japan. With the exception of a few special varieties, fresh shoots are available only for a very short period between March and April. They are prized for their rich aroma and crunchy texture. Canned bamboo shoots are peeled and boiled before packing, so they have a softer texture and less flavor than fresh ones.

Before using canned shoots, wash them well to remove the white calcium deposits, and boil to eliminate the characteristic odor.

BONITO FLAKES, THREADS, AND POWDER

Bonito flakes and kelp (*konbu*) are the two principal ingredients of Japanese bonito stock (*dashi*). Originally, flakes and threads were shaved daily from a rock-hard piece of dried bonito (top) that had been smoked, dried, and fermented over a 4-month period. Naturally, the very best bonito stock is still made from freshly shaved flakes (top right), but today most home cooks have succumbed to convenience and rely on packaged flakes. Dried bonito can also be used as a condiment. Threads (bottom left) and powder (bottom right) both fill this role, though flakes may be substituted.

When selecting flakes, look for those that are neatly shaved and have a lighter color and a good aroma. Threads should be thin and long and slightly moist; and again, the lighter the better. Bonito powder appears in Savory Pancake (page 128). Store all dried bonito products in an airtight container and refrigerate. They keep about 3 weeks once opened.

CELLOPHANE NOODLES

Cellophane noodles (*harusame*) are made from the starch of potatoes. In their dried form, they have the appearance of shredded cellophane, but when soaked in lukewarm water before using, they become transparent. Cellophane noodles will "melt" if overcooked, so keep an eye on them. There is also a Chinese version of cellophane noodles. Most of these are made of bean starch, and so they stand up to a longer simmering. The Chinese variety has a firmer texture than that of the Japanese variety. Both varieties are suitable for the recipes in this book.

CLOUD EAR MUSHROOMS

Cloud ear mushrooms look like pieces of heavyweight paper that have been frilled and crumpled. They are almost always sold dried. In selecting them, check to make sure that they are well dried. The darker the color, the better the quality is. They should be stored in a well-sealed jar or can and kept away from moisture. Usually, they are used more for their dark color and crunchy texture than for flavor. When soaked, they swell to 2 or 3 times their dehydrated size. Dried Chinese cloud ear mushrooms (right) are smaller and thinner than those produced in Japan, but swell to almost 10 times their own dried size. The number of mushrooms called for in the recipes in this book is based on the Chinese variety, which is easier to obtain in the United States. When using the larger Japanese cloud ear, quantities should be halved.

CUCUMBERS

Japanese cucumbers are much smaller than the American variety, averaging 1 inch (3 cm) in diameter and 6 to 8 inches (15–20 cm) in length. The Japanese variety offers a softer skin, fewer seeds, firmer flesh, and a crunchier texture. Select the youngest and smallest. The skin should be firm and have a fresh-looking green color.

DAIKON RADISH

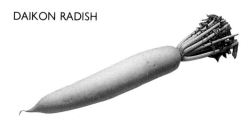

Daikon are large, heavy radishes about 15 to 20 inches (38–50 cm) long and 3 to 5 inches (8–13 cm) in diameter. They find wide use in both Japanese and Chinese cuisine. Grated, this radish is often served as a condiment or mixed into dipping sauces. Its popularity in this guise can be explained not only by its comparatively mild taste for a radish, but also by the fact that daikon contain enzymes that aid digestion and help to counteract strong, oily flavors. Select firm and shiny radishes with unscarred skins. If the leaves are still attached, choose those radishes with unwilted leaves. Both the flavor and the active enzymes diminish quickly after grating, so do this at the last possible moment. Whether grating or slicing the radish, remove the skin in thick peels, making sure to also cut away the fibers that run along the inner surface of the skin. To store, remove the leaves and wrap the whole daikon in plastic wrap. It will keep in the refrigerator for as long as 1 week.

EGGPLANTS

The most commonly used eggplants in Japan measure 1½ to 2 inches (4–5 cm) in diameter and 5 to 8 inches (13–20 cm) in length. They are similar to what are called Italian or Chinese eggplants in the United States, and 4 to 5 are approximately equivalent to 1 American eggplant. In either case, choose those that are firm to the touch and have taut skins and hard stems. Larger eggplants with tough skins should be peeled before use.

ENOKI MUSHROOMS

These tiny mushrooms have caps that are only about ¼ inch (½ cm) in diameter, and are usually about 4 to 5 inches (10–13 cm) long. In selecting *enoki* mushrooms, choose those that are white and crisp. If they have turned a brownish yellow color, they are old. The brown portion at the base of the stems should be cut away and discarded. They will keep for only 1 or 2 days if covered in plastic wrap and refrigerated.

GINGER, FRESH

Powdered ginger is avoided in Japanese cuisine because the fragrance and flavor of fresh ginger is highly prized. Fresh ginger should be hard and have a taut, unwrinkled skin. Cut off just the portion you will be using and wrap the rest in plastic wrap. It will keep in the refrigerator for 2 to 3 weeks. Cut rather deeply when peeling to remove the hard fibers running beneath the skin. When grating, it is best to grate against the grain. On the other hand, ginger slivers will be crisper if you cut with the grain.

To make ginger juice, wash the root well and peel, then grate finely over a small bowl lined with cheesecloth; squeeze the juice from the gratings.

GINGER, RED VINEGARED

Traditionally, red vinegared ginger is made by pickling fresh ginger in salt and then pickling it again in the red vinegar reserved from making pickled plums. Today, however, the bright color is almost always produced with food coloring. The ginger's sweet, vinegary taste, tart fragrance, and bright red color make it a favorite condiment for popular snacks such as Savory Pancake (page 128).

GINGER, SWEET-VINEGARED

When ginger is pickled in salt and then again in sweet vinegar, it naturally turns a pale pink. Sweet-vinegared ginger is mainly served alongside sushi and eaten to refresh the palate. It should have a natural pink color, and the fibers should not be too hard. Once opened, store-bought ginger keeps 3 to 6 months refrigerated in its own vinegar.

GINKGO NUTS

The fruit of the ginkgo tree is inedible, but the hard seed inside contains a delicious nut that is prized for its bittersweet flavor and chewy texture. It is also rich in carotene. Crack the shell open with the blunt edge of a knife. If the recipe calls for deep-frying the nuts, remove the brown skin before deep-frying. When used in boiled or simmered dishes, the nuts may be parboiled first to facilitate the removal of the skin (see page 141)

GREEN SEAWEED FLAKES

This bright green seaweed (*ao-nori*) should not be confused with *nori* seaweed. The seaweed is dried and sold in flaked or powdered form. Green seaweed flakes have their own distinctive fragrance and are used primarily as a condiment. They should be stored in a tightly sealed can to keep out moisture.

GRILLED EEL

Grilled Japanese eel (*unagi kabayaki*) is extremely popular in Japan. The eel is cut open along the spine, the bones are removed, and the flesh broiled. The secret of grilled eel is in the basting sauce. It is very difficult for the nonprofessional to make good grilled eel, so it is usually purchased precooked. In the United States, precooked eel is available at Japanese markets in the frozen foods section, or in vacuum packs.

GROUND *SANSHO* PEPPER

Sansho is unique to Japan and China. It is hot and spicy and has an extremely strong fragrance. Because the shape of the seeds and its size closely resemble those of black pepper, it is often called Japanese pepper. In fact, it is an entirely different spice. In Japanese cuisine, *sansho* is used as an herb as well as a spice: in spring, the buds are used; in early summer, the flowers; and in summer, the green seeds. In the fall, the hulls of the ripe seeds are dried and powdered to be used as a spice. The young buds are indispensable as herbs in spring dishes such as fresh bamboo shoots or clam soup. Since fresh *sansho* is rare outside Asia, we have omitted it from the recipes in this dish, but by all means try it if you have the chance. Powdered *sansho* is widely available in sealed packages and is a popular spice for Yakitori (page 60) and red miso soup. Sealed in an airtight container, it keeps in the refrigerator for 3 to 4 months.

HOT YELLOW MUSTARD

Hot yellow mustard is used throughout the world, but there are some differences between the Japanese variety and those of Europe and the United States. Japanese yellow mustard (*karashi*) is usually sold in powdered form (top) and is prepared for use in much the same way as powdered *wasabi*. Mix small quantities of powdered *karashi* and lukewarm water (about 100° F/45° C) in a small dish and cover for 10 minutes until the characteristic zesty smell is noticeable. Once it is mixed with water, *karashi* cannot be stored. The flavor and sharpness disappear quickly. Sealed in an airtight container, powdered *karashi* keeps in the refrigerator for 3 to 4 months. *Karashi* paste (left) sold in tubes is also available but is inferior to powdered *karashi*: oil and salt have been added, and the aroma is much less distinctive. Any mustard that is not sweet or vinegary makes a fine substitute, but European hot mustards to which vinegar, wine, salt, and various other ingredients have been added are best avoided.

INSTANT BONITO STOCK

Bonito stock can be prepared much more easily than stock for French or Chinese cuisine, but a number of instant products are available in both liquid and powdered form. These combine powdered dried bonito, essence of *konbu* kelp, monosodium glutamate (MSG), salt, and sugar. To make bonito stock, see page 140.

KELP

Dried kelp (*konbu*) joins bonito flakes as one of the two main ingredients of bonito stock (*dashi*), Japanese-style soup stock. There are many varieties of *konbu*, but in its natural state it may vary from 1 to 12 inches (3–30 cm) in width and 1½ to 20 yards (1.5–20 m) in length. The best dried kelp has a dark, greenish brown color, a thick flesh, and a fine white powder on the surface. After purchase, it should be stored in a sealed jar or can to keep out moisture. The white powder on the surface provides one of the flavors of dried kelp and should not be washed off. Before using, wipe the surface lightly with a damp cloth to remove any foreign matter.

KELP, SALTED

This processed kelp product uses the highest-quality kelp. Before drying, it is boiled for a long time in soy sauce. As the kelp dries, the salt solidifies on the surface, covering it with a white powder. Usually, salted kelp (*shio-konbu*) is sold in 1-inch (2-cm) squares; the best salted *konbu* is thick and completely covered with salt. It can be stored for a considerable length of time in a tightly sealed container, but it spoils quickly if exposed to moisture.

KONNYAKU

Made from *konnyaku* potatoes (devil's tongue), *konnyaku* has the consistency of a tough gelatin. Since it

is almost tasteless, it is used mainly for its texture. A low flavor-absorbing ability and characteristic odor in fresh *konnyaku* are usually countered with a short parboiling. *Konnyaku* commonly comes in blocks about the same size as tofu cakes, and in both unrefined and refined forms, "black" and "white." Flavored *konnyaku* with hot red pepper, sesame seeds, or green seaweed flakes is also available. Various types of *konnyaku* noodles are also available in Japan, and they are extremely popular in Sukiyaki (page 122) and other one-pot dishes. If they are available, we highly recommend trying them. Refrigerated in ample water to cover, *konnyaku* cakes or noodles keep for as long as 2 weeks if the water is changed once a day.

MIRIN

Mirin is a sweet, artificially manufactured liquor made from rice and distilled alcohol. It has an alcohol content of about 14 percent. Originally a beverage, *mirin* is now used almost exclusively for cooking. As a sweetener, it is milder than sugar; as a kitchen staple, it is effective in firming up the flesh of meats and fish during cooking. In broiling, it produces a pleasing amber color and a high gloss. When *mirin* is unavailable, use sugar and halve the quantity by volume.

When cooking continues for a lengthy time after the *mirin* has been added, the alcohol will burn off naturally, but when it is to be added toward the end, or when a large quantity is to be used, the alcohol should be burned off by heating the *mirin* in a saucepan, igniting it, and letting the flame burn itself out.

MISO PASTE

This uniquely Japanese flavoring ingredient is made by fermenting a mixture of soybeans, a fermenting agent (rice, barley, or soy *koji*), salt, and water. Every local area in Japan has its own miso paste, so numerous varieties exist. Color ranges along a spectrum from something near ivory to a dark amber, and the salt content varies from about 3 to 15 percent. Miso can be compared to cheese in that two varieties may appear similar to the eye, but in fact have completely different flavors, aromas, and degrees of mellowness. The following is a brief explanation of the three most typical varieties.

Sweet white miso (top): From ivory to light beige in color, this type of miso is made by using rice *koji* spores and keeping the fermentation time short. White miso usually has a sweet, mellow taste and a relatively low salt content. But in miso soup, the

most common miso dish, about 1⅓ Tbsps (20 g) are used for each serving, compared to ⅔–1 Tbsp (10–15 g) for the other two types. Partly because of its low salt content, sweet white miso does not travel well, so it is rarely exported. For this reason, we have not used it in any of the recipes in this book. In fact, however, it is superior to nonsweet white miso for dressings.

Nonsweet white miso (left): This type includes varieties of miso from yellowish brown to brown in color. Either rice or barley *koji* may be used in making this type, and a proportionately greater quantity of soybeans is used than in sweet white miso. It is also aged longer, so unlike sweet white miso it travels well and is commonly marketed abroad. It has a somewhat higher salt content than sweet miso. Referring again to the example of miso soup, only ⅔–1 Tbsp (10–15 g) is required for each serving.

Red miso (bottom right): From pale to dark amber in color, this type of miso is produced by using soybean *koji* and allowing the miso to mature for a long period (it has the longest aging period of the three types). Red miso has a rich taste and aroma, a light touch of acidity and astringency, and a very high salt content. However, what is sold as red miso today has almost always been blended with one of the other types. Here, too, ⅔–1 Tbsp (10–15 g) is used in preparing a single serving of miso soup.

If placed in an airtight container and refrigerated, miso paste will keep about 3 months.

NORI SEAWEED

Anyone who has eaten rolled sushi will be familiar with these paper-thin sheets of dried seaweed. The best *nori* has a bright sheen, a dark, blackish purple color with a hint of green, and a good aroma. It should be stored in a tightly sealed can to keep out moisture and sunlight. Besides the standard-sized sheets, precut strips of toasted *nori* and flavored *nori* are also marketed. It is better, though, to use standard-sized sheets and toast them yourself just before using. When *nori* is toasted over direct heat, it releases a distinctive fragrance and its color quickly changes to a shiny dark green. (To toast, see page 143.)

PEPPERS, SMALL SWEET GREEN

With diameters of about ½ inch (1 cm) and lengths of 2 to 3 inches (5–8 cm), these skinny sweet peppers are much smaller than bell peppers. The flesh is thinner and there are fewer seeds, so peppers can be eaten whole except for the stem. They are particularly rich in carotene. Like the Western green pepper, they are available the year round. Select these small peppers for their firmness and a bright green color.

PICKLED PLUMS

Plums contain relatively large amounts of acid and when they are pickled in salt the result is an extremely salty and acidic flavor that produces a distinctive sensation on the palate. Pickling takes place in the plum season in early and midsummer. *Shiso* is also in season at this time, so red *shiso* is frequently added to color plums a bright red. Pickled plums (*umeboshi*) can be eaten after about six months, but it is often said that the taste is smoother if they are allowed to pickle for at least a full year. Store in a cool, dark place.

RICE

Boiled rice is the main staple of Japanese cuisine. It is most often eaten plain, and less frequently served topped with a mélange of egg and vegetables or some such, or vinegared to make sushi; occasionally other ingredients are mixed into the rice and boiled with it. Like bread, its wide range of applications makes it the ideal staple. The rice cultivated in Japan is of the short-grain variety (left), which is also grown in other regions with temperate climates. Boiled, it has a soft, sticky texture. The long-grain rice (right) grown in tropical regions is crunchier and does not have this stickiness. Though not suitable for dishes like pilaf, short-grain rice is perfect for sushi or rice balls, the quintessential Japanese snacks, or as a complement to most of the dishes presented in this book.

When purchasing rice, check the date of harvest to find the newest rice possible. Rice should be selected for its plumpness, a near transparent color, and the brightness of the grains. When cooking rice (see page 101), special attention should be given to washing the rice well but quickly, using the correct proportion of rice to water, and adjusting the level of heat.

RICE CAKES

Glutinous rice is used in making rice cakes (*mochi*). The rice is soaked and steamed, then crushed into a mash and formed into round or square cakes of various sizes. Dried rice cakes are also available. Grilled and sprinkled with soy sauce or sugar, they are a popular snack. They may also be used in soups and are widely used in making Japanese confections.

RICE VINEGAR

Every country has its national drink, and the same ingredients are almost always used in brewing its vinegar. In Japan, rice is the main shared ingredient. The acidic flavor of rice vinegar is milder than that of wine or apple vinegar. It has a sweet aroma and a rich, mellow flavor. Neither wine nor apple vinegar can be substituted for rice vinegar in Japanese cuisine. Wine vinegar is not sufficiently sweet, and apple vinegar has an aroma that is too strong for delicate Japanese dishes. Even among the various Japanese brands on the market, it is important to avoid those that are not pure fermented rice vinegar. They are too acidic and lack full flavor.

SAKÉ

Saké is not only Japan's national drink, but an important ingredient in Japanese cuisine. Its basic ingredients are rice, a fermenting agent (rice *koji*), and water. It is brewed by employing a unique technique called parallel multiple fermentation. At 18 to 20 percent, the alcohol content of undiluted saké is the highest of any fermented beverage. Most sakés on the market, however, have been diluted and have an alcohol content of 14 to 17 percent.

In cooking, saké tenderizes meat or fish and eliminates strong or acidic flavors. It increases the ability of ingredients to absorb flavors and at the same time draws out the flavors and subtle undertones of the ingredients. Moreover, it contributes its own unique flavor as a "hidden touch" and adds a glossy finish to dishes. It is not necessary to use the very finest saké in cooking. The least-expensive bottle of one of the major Japanese brands will do nicely. Saké deteriorates fairly quickly after opening, so buy smaller bottles and use within 3 months.

To burn off the alcohol, heat the saké in a saucepan, ignite, and wait until the flame burns itself out.

SALMON ROE

Ikura, the Russian word for fish roe, is used in the Japanese language to refer to salmon roe that has been separated into individual pea-shaped eggs and salted. Though most familiar as a popular delicacy at sushi bars, salmon roe, with its brilliant orange color, also makes an ideal topping for canapés and other Western-style appetizers. Choose roe with taut, unwrinkled skin and avoid any packages that include broken eggs.

SEA URCHIN

Not a mollusk but an echinoderm, sea urchins can be found along coastlines throughout the world. There are many varieties, and the type that can be harvested commercially varies from region to region. The most common variety in Japan resembles a black, spiny ball and carries about 6 bright orange egg sacs, each about 1 inch (3 cm) long. Sold and kept in small wooden boxes, sea urchin is enormously popular in sushi bars and is considered to be a delicacy. It is almost always eaten fresh, though it is sometimes pickled in salt or alcohol and sold in bottles. Fresh sea urchin roe should have well-defined edges and should look firm, not runny. Sea urchin spoils very quickly and should be eaten as soon after purchase as possible.

SESAME SEEDS

Prized for their rich taste and aroma, sesame seeds are used in cuisines throughout the world. There are white, black, and brown varieties, but white and black are the most commonly used. Sesame seeds should be selected for roundness and plumpness. In order to bring out their flavor and aroma, they should always be toasted (page 140) before using. Black sesame seeds are used mainly in recipes that highlight the shape and color of the seeds. White sesame may also be used in this way, but in general it is employed in dressings and condiments, chopped, crushed, or ground after toasting.

SEVEN-SPICE PEPPER

As its name suggests, this pepper (*shichimi*) is a combination of seven spices. It is a favorite seasoning for Yakitori (page 60), broiled meats or fish, and hot noodle dishes. There are no hard and fast conventions for the mixture, but usually two hot spices and five aromatic ones are chosen from a repertoire of dried spices that includes hemp seeds, dried tangerine-peel flakes, sesame seeds, poppy seeds, green seaweed flakes (*ao-nori*), green *shiso*, red *shiso*, *shiso* seeds, hot Chinese peppers, *sansho* pepper, and ginger. The most typical mixture combines flax seeds, dried tangerine-peel flakes, sesame seeds, poppy seeds, green *nori* (or green *shiso*), hot Chinese pepper, and *sansho* pepper.

147

SHIITAKE MUSHROOMS

Highly prized for its rich aroma, the shiitake, or Chinese black mushroom, is the most commonly used mushroom in Japanese cuisine. The average shiitake has a cap measuring 2 inches (5 cm) in diameter. In selecting fresh mushrooms, choose those that have dark brown caps, white undersides, and tucked edges. Like champignons, fresh shiitake mushrooms can be stored for only 2 to 3 days and should be covered with plastic wrap and refrigerated.

Dried shiitake mushrooms should be selected for their brown caps and a cracked appearance and should also be thoroughly dried. Well-cracked caps and very thick flesh indicate high quality. Dried shiitake have a much stronger aroma and flavor than fresh ones and so are preferred in simmered dishes and such when a rich flavor is desired. When they are soaked, much of their savory flavor disperses into the water, so the soaking water itself may be added to simmering liquid or whatever. Dried shiitake, found in either Japanese or Chinese specialty stores, keep indefinitely stored in an airtight container.

SHIMEJI MUSHROOMS AND OYSTER MUSHROOMS

Three different types of mushrooms are sold in Japan as shimeji. Aside from the "genuine" article, both shiro-tamogi (left) and oyster mushrooms (right) are marketed as shimeji to fill the void left by the scarcity of the real article. The two "impostors" are harmless enough, but the distinction should be made. For practical purposes, since real shimeji rarely reach common outlets, either of the other two must suffice, and in this book, we have adopted the common convention throughout, referring to shiro-tamogi as shimeji.

Both the alternatives are cultivated and available throughout the year. Shimeji mushrooms (that is, shiro-tamogi) should be selected for their light brown color, plump round caps, and thick white stems. Oyster mushrooms should have grayish brown caps and thick, white stems. Both varieties are usually sold in clumps with the stem buried in a thick layer of root at the bottom. Some of this layer should be removed and the clumps separated into several smaller groups. The mushrooms will stay fresh for only 2 or 3 days and should be kept in the refrigerator, wrapped in plastic.

SHISO LEAVES

Shiso belongs to the same family as mint and basil, but its fragrance is completely different. It is one of the unique herbs of Japanese cuisine. Both red and green shiso are produced in Japan, but the red variety is used primarily as a coloring agent in Japanese pickles. Green shiso is most common as a garnish or condiment. In Japan, not only the leaves, but also the buds, flowers, and seeds are used to give a seasonal touch to dishes. Rich in calcium and iron, shiso was originally employed as a medicine and preservative.

SOBA NOODLES

Soba noodles are made from buckwheat (soba) flour, light wheat flour, salt, and water. It is kneaded and cut into long, thin noodles that have a grayish brown color. The noodles are less elastic than udon noodles. Like udon, packaged soba is available fresh (top), precooked (left), or dried (bottom right). Dried noodles are the most convenient and can be stored in a cool, dry place for about 1 year. Fresh or precooked noodles keep, at most, 3 days if sealed in plastic wrap and refrigerated.

SOMEN NOODLES

The dough for somen noodles is made from hard (bread) flour, salt, and water. After it is kneaded, the dough is cut into thick "ropes," which are then covered lightly with oil and stretched until they reach a diameter of only $\frac{1}{32}$ of an inch (about 1 mm). These thin "strings" are dried and then cut into short noodles. Today, both hand- and machine-stretched noodles are sold, the former, of course, having the superior texture and flavor. Somen noodles should be selected for their gloss. Store them in a tightly sealed can and place them in a cool, dry place.

SOYBEANS, FRESH YOUNG

Young soybeans, or edamame (literally "branch beans"), are a favorite summer snack for the Japanese. The bright green pods are boiled in salted water and served just as they are. The beans pop out of their casing when pressed, so they are a perfect snack food. Young soybeans are harder than green peas or fava beans and have a distinctive sweetness. The pods should be bright green, and the tiny hairs covering them should be short. Bulging pods indicate that the beans inside are fat and tender. Wrapped in clear plastic wrap, they keep for 2 to 3 days if refrigerated. Frozen beans are also available.

SOY SAUCE

An indispensable flavoring ingredient in Japanese cuisine, soy sauce is produced by fermenting a mixture of soybeans, wheat, salt, and water. Besides its saltiness, soy sauce has a distinctive aroma and a mellow sweetness. A number of types are available in Japan, but the following explanation is limited to those that appear in this book.

Dark soy sauce (top): With its beautiful dark brown color, its fruity aroma, and sweet, mellow flavor, dark soy sauce is by far the most popular soy sauce in Japan. It has a salt content of slightly less than 18 percent.

Light soy sauce (left): Slightly saltier than dark soy sauce, this type is fermented for a shorter period to achieve a lighter color and to bring out the flavors of the ingredients. The addition of a sweet drink called amazake during fermentation results in a milder flavor and aroma.

Tamari soy sauce (right): This type of soy sauce is black with a touch of amber and has a viscous quality. It has a rich, deep flavor and a distinctive, sweet aroma. These effects are achieved by using almost no wheat and the longest fermenting time of the three types.

In addition to the above three types, low-salt soy sauce with a salt content below 10 percent has recently been developed for people who must restrict their intake of salt.

Once soy sauce is opened, its color quickly darkens and its flavor weakens, so it is best to buy it in quantities that you know you will use quickly. It can be stored at room temperature, but it is better to refrigerate it.

SQUID

There are many species of squid, each with its own characteristic shape and color. Squid can be roughly divided into those that have an internal shell, or cuttlebone, and those that have only the spiny quill running the length of their body sacs. Squid should be selected principally for the thickness of the body meat—the thicker the better. Fresh ones will have flesh that appears almost transparent, and will be firm to the touch. Another way to check for freshness is to touch the suckers. You should be able to feel a mild sucking sensation. Clean the squid (see page 141) as soon after purchase as possible, then cover it in plastic wrap and refrigerate until ready to use. Ideally, squid should be eaten on the day of purchase. The flavor is relatively unchanged by freezing, so quick-frozen squid is widely available. Be careful not to overcook squid. Prepare it with a brisk, light touch, and stop before the meat becomes tough and rubbery.

TOFU, FREEZE-DRIED

Freeze-dried tofu (*Koya-dofu*, *kori-dofu*, or *shimi-dofu*) has a distinctive spongy texture that sets it apart from fresh tofu. Rich in protein, fat, and calcium, it is an ideal healthfood. The traditional method of making it took advantage of the cold of winter to freeze-dry the tofu outdoors. Today, of course, it is produced in large freezing units, giving us a tofu that is simpler to reconstitute than naturally freeze-dried tofu. Nevertheless, how it is reconstituted (see page 81) still has a considerable influence on the taste, so keep an eye on the temperature and time. And since freeze-dried tofu has the characteristic odor common to many dried foods, it should be thoroughly rinsed after soaking.

TOFU, FRESH

Tofu is one of the most popular traditional processed foods of China and Japan. In cooking, it is important to note that Japanese tofu is softer and smoother than the Chinese variety. There are two basic types of Japanese tofu, the standard "cotton" type (left) and the "silk" variety (right). Cotton tofu is firmer and has a rough surface. Slicing open the cake reveals the "grain" of the tofu. The silk type has a soft, glossy surface and is perfect for dishes that call for ingredients with a smooth, delicate texture. Both types contain exactly the same ingredients, only the way the tofu is made differs.

To make cotton tofu, dried soybeans are soaked in water until they swell to their original size, then they are crushed and steamed to make a mash. The mash is strained to yield a smooth tofu milk. When this is mixed with a coagulating agent it forms a curd, which is packed into shallow wooden molds. The molds used for cotton-type tofu have holes and are covered with cloth so some of the moisture drains away, leaving a pocked, cragged surface. Weight is applied from above until the curd firms up and becomes tofu. The technique of making silk tofu is only slightly different. The molds do not have holes and no weight is applied while the tofu is firming. The tofu milk is brought to a thicker consistency and poured directly into the molds as soon as the coagulant has been added. In both cases, the tofu is removed in a block from the mold and submerged in a large tub of water. In the neighborhood tofu shop in Japan, huge tanks of clean water hold these large blocks of fresh tofu, from which the small cakes are then cut.

After purchasing, it is essential to place the tofu in water deep enough to cover it. Cakes can be kept in

the refrigerator for up to two days, if the water is changed at least twice a day, but like many fresh foods it is best eaten on the day of purchase.

TOFU, THICK DEEP-FRIED

Thick deep-fried tofu (*atsuage* or *namaage*) is made by deep-frying 1-inch (3-cm) thick slabs in very hot oil until the surface is golden brown. The inside should still be soft and white. Unlike thin deep-fried tofu (see next entry), this thick version cannot be frozen, and lasts under the best conditions—that is, covered in plastic wrap and refrigerated—only 1 or 2 days. Like thin deep-fried tofu, it should be blanched before use. It comes in several shapes and sizes.

TOFU, THIN DEEP-FRIED

Thin deep-fried tofu (*usuage*, *aburaage*, or *aburage*) is made by deep-frying thin slices of tofu until they turn golden brown. Sealed in plastic wrap, it keeps 1 week refrigerated, or 2 to 3 months frozen. The secret to using thin deep-fried tofu is to blanch it first to remove excess oil. It is sold in various shapes and sizes.

UDON NOODLES

Udon noodles are made by making a dough of all-purpose flour, water, and salt. This is then kneaded and cut into long, thin noodles. Packaged *udon* is sold fresh (top), precooked (left), or dried (bottom right). The noodles vary in thickness from ⅛ to ¼ inch (¼–½ cm) and may be square, round, or flat. Since all-purpose flour is used, *udon* is not as firm as spaghetti, but it should still have a firm elasticity after boiling. Dried *udon* is the most convenient to use and can be stored in a cool, dry place for about 1 year. Its only drawback is that the noodles tend to be a little hard. Naturally, fresh *udon* has a better fragrance and texture than either precooked or dried *udon*. Use it if it is available. Sealed in plastic wrap,

fresh or precooked *udon* can be kept in the refrigerator for as long as 3 days.

WAKAME SEAWEED

Wakame seaweed is extremely popular in Japan for its delightfully smooth texture and its special fragrance. Rich in calcium, it is a superb healthfood. In Japan, fresh *wakame* appears on the market only in the spring, but dried *wakame* is available all year round. Due to differences in drying methods, there are a number of varieties, but in every case the best *wakame* should have a dark, blackish green color. *Wakame* is extremely delicate, and overcooking will cause the pieces of seaweed to "melt." (To reconstitute and prepare, see page 143.)

WASABI HORSERADISH

An indispensable condiment for sashimi or *Nigiri* Sushi (page 110), *wasabi* is a uniquely Japanese spice. Genuine *wasabi* is made by grating the root of the *wasabi* plant (top left). It has a light, fruity smell and a tingling hotness that goes straight to the nose. The best *wasabi* roots are fat and moist. Black spots on the stem or leaves are a sure sign that the *wasabi* is past its peak of freshness. After peeling, grate the root, top end first, over a fine surface in a circular motion. The sharpness and fragrance of the *wasabi* will disappear quickly after grating, so it is best to prepare it at the last moment. Grate only what you will be using and wrap the rest in wet paper before covering with plastic wrap. The root can be used until it begins to soften and droop. Grated *wasabi* can also be wrapped and kept for an extended period in the freezer (though it will lose some of its zestiness).

Outside Japan, *wasabi* is rare and expensive. Even in Japan fresh *wasabi* is extremely expensive, for it can only be cultivated in clean running water, so powdered (top right) or "tubed" (bottom) *wasabi* is the norm. They use a combination of Western horseradish and *wasabi* and hot oil with an artificial green coloring. Powdered *wasabi* is another alternative and is prepared by mixing briskly with water until it reaches a paste. It should be covered and allowed to set for about 10 minutes before serving.

INDEX

Abalone, 144
  Steamed Abalone, 14
almonds
  Almond Dressing, 65
appetizers, 8–19
  Beef Salad, 57
  Rolled Beef and Asparagus, 56
  Sardines Simmered with Ginger, 36
  Yakitori, 60
asparagus
  Rolled Beef and Asparagus, 56
  in Rolled Flounder with Egg, 11
  Squid and Asparagus with Mustard-Miso Sauce, 19
  in Thick Roll Sushi, 113
  in Vegetable-and-Shrimp Clusters, 87
avocado
  Endive Boats with Avocado, Crab, and Salmon Roe, 18
  as possible ingredient, 65

Bamboo rolling mats, 143
bamboo shoots, 144
  Simmered Bamboo Shoot with *Wakame* Seaweed, 92
  in Simmered Rockfish, 32
beef, 50–57
  in Deep-Fried Mixed Kebabs, 132
  in *Oden* Stew, 124
  in Sukiyaki, 122
  as possible ingredient, 34, 82
bento. See box meals.
bonito
  Quick-Seared Bonito Sashimi, 26
bonito flakes, threads, and powder, 144
bonito stock
  instant, 146
  preparation of, 140
box meals, 134–39
broccoli
  in Freeze-Dried Tofu with Egg, 81
broths
  bonito stock, 140, 146
  chicken stock, 22
butterfish
  Yuan-Style Grilled Butterfish, 34

Cabbage. *See also* Chinese cabbage.
  in Savory Pancake, 128
celery
  Sautéed Celery with Sesame, 94
cellophane noodles, 144
  in Deep-Fried Flounder Boat, 30
  in Deep-Fried Stuffed Pork, 59
  in Seafood Pot, 126
cheese
  in Deep-Fried Mixed Kebabs, 132
  in Deep-Fried Stuffed Pork, 59
  as possible ingredient, 86
chicken, 60–65
  Chicken and Egg on Rice, 101
  Chicken Ball and Cucumber Soup, 22
  Night-Dried Tofu with Chicken Sauce, 72
  in *Oden* Stew, 124
  in Seafood Pot, 126
  in Stuffed Cabbage, Japanese Style, 91
  Stuffed Minced-Chicken Rolls, 12
  in *Udon* Pot, 118
  in White Salad, 77
Chinese cabbage
  Chinese Cabbage and Deep-Fried Tofu, 90
  Stuffed Cabbage, Japanese Style, 91
clams
  Clam Soup, 22

Clams Grilled in the Shell, 45
  in Seafood Pot, 126
  in *Udon* Pot, 118
corn
  Pureed Corn Soup, 24
crab
  Crab Ball Soup, 20
  Endive Boats with Avocado, Crab, and Salmon Roe, 18
  Vinegared Crab, 46
  as possible ingredient, 91
cucumbers, 144
  Chicken Ball and Cucumber Soup, 22
  Skewered Omelette, Cucumber, and Shrimp, 10

Daikon radish, 144
  in Red Maple Radish, 140
dashi. See bonito stock.
dipping sauces. *See also* sauces.
  Lemon-Soy Dipping Sauce (*Ponzu*), 27, 31, 50, 52
  Sesame Dipping Sauce, 50
  Soy-Bonito Dipping Sauce, 32
  for Tempura, 130
  Tosa Dipping Sauce, 28, 29
dressings. *See* salad dressings.
drop-lids, 143
duck
  Sautéed Duck Breast with Sauce, 13
  Soba Noodles with Duck, 121
  as possible ingredient, 24, 34, 50, 56, 100

Eel, grilled, 145
  in Steamed Grated Turnip, 88
  in sushi, 110
eggplants, 145
  Deep-Fried Eggplant Sandwiches, 86
  Deep-Fried Eggplant with Miso Sauce, 85
  Grilled Eggplant, 84
Eggs, 66–69
  Chicken and Egg on Rice, 101
  Freeze-Dried Tofu with Egg, 81
  in *Oden* Stew, 124
  Okra and Coddled Egg with *Wasabi* Sauce, 97
  Rolled Flounder with Egg, 11
  Skewered Omelette, Cucumber, and Shrimp, 10
  in sushi, 104, 106, 110, 113
  Thick Omelette, 10
  Thin Omelette, 106

Fish, 26–39. *See also* white-fleshed fish.
flounder. *See also* white-fleshed fish.
  Deep-Fried Flounder Boat, 30
  Rolled Flounder with Egg, 11

Ginger, 145
  Ginger-Miso Sauce, 88
  Ginger-Vinegar Dressing, 46
  Sardines Simmered with Ginger, 36
ginkgo nuts, 145
  in Jade Green Deep-Fried Shrimp, 19
  preparation, 141
  in Steamed Grated Turnip, 88
gourd ribbons
  in sushi, 106, 113, 115
green peppers, 146
  Grilled Squid with Golden Topping and Oil-Grilled Green Peppers, 16
green seaweed flakes, 145

Kanpyo. See gourd ribbons.
kelp, 146
kiwi fruit
  Scallops and Kiwi Fruit with Three-Flavors Dressing, 49

as possible ingredient, 65
konnyaku, 146
  in *Oden* Stew, 124
  preparation, 142
  in Sukiyaki, 122
  as possible ingredient, 94

Leeks
  Shrimps and Leeks with Mustard-Miso Sauce, 48
lobster
  Saké-Simmered Lobster, 42
  Stuffed Spiny Lobster, 40

Mackerel
  Simmered Mackerel in Miso, 37
  in sushi, 108, 110
marinades
  for beef, 56
  for chicken, 63, 64
  for fish, 11, 34, 104, 108, 110
  for vegetables, 96
mirin, 146
miso paste, 146
  Ginger-Miso Sauce, 88
  Grilled Beef with Miso, 54
  Miso Soup with Pork and Vegetables, 25
  Mustard-Miso Sauce, 19, 48
  in Pureed Corn Soup, 24
  Red Miso Sauce, 85
  Simmered Mackerel in Miso, 37
  in Tofu Hamburger Steak, 80
  as possible ingredient, 40
mochi. See rice cakes.
mushrooms. *See also* shiitake mushrooms.
  cloud ear mushrooms, 142, 144
  enoki mushrooms, 145
  oyster mushrooms, 148
  shimeji mushrooms, 16, 148
mustard, hot yellow, 145
  Mustard-Miso Sauce, 19, 48

Noodles, 116–21. *See also* cellophane noodles.
  cooking, 118
  soba noodles, 120, 121, 148
  somen noodles, 116, 148
  udon noodles, 118, 120, 149
nori seaweed, 146
  with rice balls, 98
  with sushi, 104–7, 110, 113
  toasting, 143

Okra
  Okra and Coddled Egg with *Wasabi* Sauce, 97
one-pot dishes, 122–27
  Simmered Tofu, 70
  Udon Pot, 118

Pancakes
  Savory Pancake, 128
persimmon
  as possible ingredient, 88
pickled plums, 147
  in rice balls, 98
Ponzu Sauce. *See* dipping sauces.
pork
  in Deep-Fried Mixed Kebabs, 132
  Deep-Fried Stuffed Pork, 59
  Miso Soup with Pork and Vegetables, 25
  Nagasaki-Style Braised Pork, 58
  in Savory Pancake, 128–29
  Tofu, Pork, and Vegetable Soup, 24
  as possible ingredient, 34, 39, 50, 56, 57, 82, 91
potatoes
  in *Oden* Stew, 124

Stuffed Potato Buns, 82
prawns. *See also* shrimp.
  Whole Prawns Grilled in the Shell, 42

Raw fish and meat. *See* sashimi.
rice, 147
  cooking, 101
  rice dishes, 98–101
rice cakes, 147
  in *Udon* Pot, 118
rice vinegar, 147
rockfish
  Simmered Rockfish, 32

Saké, 147
  Saké-Simmered Lobster, 42
salad dressings
  Almond Dressing, 65
  Beef-Salad dressing, 57
  Ginger-Vinegar Dressing, 46
  Sesame Dressing, 97
  Three-Flavors Dressing, 49
  Tofu Dressing, 77
  White Sesame Dressing, 96
salads
  Beef Salad, 57
  Chicken, Grapefruit, and Corn Salad with
    Almond Dressing, 65
  Marinated Watercress, 96
  Scallops and Kiwi Fruit with Three-Flavors
    Dressing, 49
  Shrimps and Leeks with Mustard-Miso Sauce, 48
  Spinach with Sesame Dressing, 97
  Squid and Asparagus with Mustard-Miso Sauce,
    19
  Vegetables with White Sesame Dressing, 96
  Vinegared Crab, 46
  White Salad, 77
salmon, fresh
  in rice balls, 98
  Stuffed Salmon, 38
salmon roe, 147
  Endive Boats with Avocado, Crab, and Salmon
    Roe, 18
salmon, smoked
  in Rolled Flounder with Egg, 11
  in sushi, 104
sardines
  Sardines Simmered with Ginger, 36
  in Scattered Sushi, 106
  Shrimp and Sardine Rafts, 17
sashimi
  Beef Tartare, Japanese Style, 52
  Paper-Thin Sea Bass Sashimi, 29
  Quick-Seared Bonito Sashimi, 26
  Scallops and Kiwi Fruit with Three-Flavors
    Dressing, 49
  Tuna Sashimi with Grated Radish, 28
sauces. *See also* dipping sauces.
  Amber Sauce, 75
  Ginger-Miso Sauce, 88
  Golden Sauce, 18
  Mustard-Miso Sauce, 19, 48
  Okonomi-yaki Sauce, 128
  Red Miso Sauce, 85
  Silver Sauce, 82
  Soy-Ginger Sauce, 84
  straining and clarifying, 142
  Teriyaki Sauce, 35, 43, 44
  tomato sauce, 80
  vegetable sauce, 39
  Wasabi Sauce, 97
  Yakitori sauce, 60–61
scallops
  in Deep-Fried Mixed Kebabs, 132
  Scallop and Vegetable Soup, 25
  Scallops and Kiwi Fruit with Three-Flavors
    Dressing, 49
  in Tempura, 130

sea bass
  Deep-Fried Sea Bass, 32
  Paper-Thin Sea Bass Sashimi, 29
sea bream
  in Seafood Pot, 126
  in sushi, 104, 108, 110
sea urchin, 147
  in Deep-Fried Mixed Kebabs, 132
  in Jellied Shrimp and Sea Urchin, 15
  with steamed abalone, 14
  in sushi, 104, 110
seaweed. *See* green seaweed flakes; kelp; *nori*
    seaweed; *wakame* seaweed.
sesame paste
  making, 140
  in Sesame Dipping Sauce, 50
  in Tofu Dressing, 77
  in White Sesame Dressing, 96
sesame seeds, 147
  Sesame Dressing, 97
  toasting, 140
seven-spice pepper. *See* spices.
shiitake mushrooms, 148
  in Chilled *Somen* Noodles, 116
  in Grilled Beef, 50
  preparation, 142
  in Seafood Pot, 126
  in Sukiyaki, 122
  in sushi, 106, 113, 115
  in Tempura, 130–31
  in *Udon* Pot, 118
  in White Salad, 77
  as possible ingredient, 86
shiso leaves, 148
shrimp. *See also* prawns.
  in Chilled *Somen* Noodles, 116
  deveining shrimp, 48
  Jade Green Deep-Fried Shrimp, 19
  Jellied Shrimp and Sea Urchin, 15
  in Savory Pancake, 128
  in Seafood Pot, 126
  Shrimp and Leeks with Mustard-Miso Sauce, 48
  Shrimp and Sardine Rafts, 17
  Skewered Omelette, Cucumber, and Shrimp, 10
  in sushi, 104, 106, 110
  in Tempura, 130
  in *Udon* Pot, 118
  Vegetable-and-Shrimp Clusters, 87
  as possible ingredient, 91
slicing fish, 29, 32
soba. *See* noodles.
somen. *See* noodles.
soups, 20–25. *See also* broths.
  straining and clarifying, 142
soybeans, 148
  Simmered Soybeans, 94
soy sauce, 148
spices
  ground *sansho* pepper, 145
  seven-spice pepper, 147
spinach
  Spinach with Sesame Dressing, 97
squash
  Deep-Fried and Simmered Acorn Squash, 93
  in Tempura, 130
squid, 148
  cleaning, 141
  in Deep-Fried Mixed Kebabs, 132
  Grilled Squid with Golden Topping and Oil-
    Grilled Green Peppers, 16
  in Savory Pancake, 128
  scoring and skewering, 44
  Squid and Asparagus with Mustard-Miso Sauce,
    19
  Squid Teriyaki, 44
  in sushi, 104, 110
  in Tempura, 130
stock. *See* broths.

sushi, 102–15
  making sushi dressing, 104
  rolling sushi, 104–5, 108–9, 113
  shaping *Nigiri* Sushi, 112
sweet potato
  in Tempura, 130
  in Vegetable-and-Shrimp Clusters, 87

Tamari soy sauce, 51 (note), 148
tataki
  Beef Tartare, Japanese Style, 52
  Quick-Seared Bonito Sashimi, 26
tempura, 130
  Vegetable-and-Shrimp Clusters, 87
teriyaki
  Squid Teriyaki, 44
  Yellowtail Teriyaki, 35
tofu, 70–81, 149
  Chinese Cabbage and Deep-Fried Tofu, 90
  in Deep-Fried and Simmered Acorn Squash, 93
  in *Oden* Stew, 124
  in Seafood Pot, 126
  in Sukiyaki, 122
  in sushi, 106, 113, 115
  Tofu Dressing, 77
  Tofu, Pork, and Vegetable Soup, 24
  Udon Noodles with Deep-Fried Tofu, 120
  in White Sesame Dressing, 96
  as possible ingredient, 38, 39, 100
tofu pulp (*okara*)
  in Nagasaki-Style Braised Pork, 58
trout
  Deep-Fried Trout in Vegetable Sauce, 39
tuna
  in sushi, 110
  Tuna Sashimi with Grated Radish, 28
turnips
  Steamed Grated Turnip, 88
  Turnip Chrysanthemum, 35, 141
  Turnip with Ginger-Miso Sauce, 88

Udon. *See* noodles.
umeboshi. *See* pickled plums.

Vegetables, 82–97. *See also* one-pot dishes; salads;
    soups.

Wakame seaweed, 149
  preparation, 143
  Simmered Bamboo Shoot with *Wakame*
    Seaweed, 92
wasabi horseradish, 149
  Wasabi Sauce, 97
watercress
  Marinated Watercress, 96
white-fleshed fish
  in Crab Ball Soup, 20
  in Decorative Sushi, 104
  in Deep-Fried Mixed Kebabs, 132
  in Night-Dried Sole, 30
  in *Oden* Stew, 124
  in Tempura, 130
  as possible ingredient, 15, 68, 73, 82, 100

Yellowtail
  in sushi, 110
  Yellowtail Teriyaki, 35

Zucchini
  Deep-Fried Zucchini, 94
  in Grilled Beef with Miso, 54
  in Simmered Tofu Dumplings, 73

151

The TSUJI Culinary Institute Group is one of the largest institutes for culinary education in the world. The schools of the group have graduated 135,000 students. At the Tsuji Culinary Institute, students learn from the basics of Japanese, French, Italian, and Chinese cooking to advanced specialized techniques in a selected major. At the Tsuji Institute of Patisserie, students may perfect their techniques of Western and Japanese confectionary and baking. The Tsuji Schools of Advanced Studies near Lyon in France, accept those desirous of completing their education with firsthand experience in Europe. In addition to its teaching facilities, the group has an editorial office, which, with various publishing firms, has jointly produced over seven hundred books, including *Etude Historique de la Cuisine Française* (in Japanese) and *Japanese Cooking: A Simple Art* (in English), both ground-breaking works in their respective language. The Tsuji Culinary Institute Group, with graduates placed in many of the restaurants in and outside Japan, is an influential force in Japan's food industry.

Shizuo Tsuji was the founder and president of the Tsuji Culinary Institute Group. He published extensively, writing the best-selling classic *Japanese Cooking: A Simple Art* and more than thirty books on gastronomy, music and travel in Japanese. Recognized by the French government for his tireless work in promoting French cuisine and culture in Japan, he was named *Meilleur Ouvrier de France* (M.O.F.) *honoris causa*. Mr. Tsuji passed away in 1993.

Koichiro Hata, ex-head of the Japanese cookery facilities at the Tsuji Culinary Institute Group, appeared regularly on nationally broadcast television programs, and wrote numerous cooking books in Japanese. He taught and lectured on Japanese food not only in his native land, but abroad as well, most notably in the United States and Asian countries.

Yoshiki Tsuji, president of the Tsuji Culinary Institute Group, has studied and researched the most recent trends in European and American cuisine and used this knowledge to educate the next generation of professional chefs. Also, he has played an active part in introducing Japanese food culture to countries outside Japan. His publications include (English translations of Japanese titles): *An Unknown World of Washoku, Secrets of Japanese Cuisine Revealed by Tsuji Culinary Institute* and *Technology of Gastronomy.*

David Bouley worked with some of Europe's leading chefs and at the finest restaurants in New York City before he opened Bouley there in 1985. After launching several more restaurants, a bakery/café, and the Bouley Test Kitchen, he collaborated with the Tsuji Culinary Institute on Brushstroke, a *kaiseki* restaurant. Recent ventures include an eight-seat sushi bar at Brushstroke and Bouley Botanical, an event space and kitchen where he grows over 400 edible plants and herbs.